HOLOCAUST RESCUERS

Ten Stories of Courage

Dedication
To my brother Dennis

Collective Biographies

HOLOCAUST RESCUERS

Ten Stories of Courage

Darryl Lyman

Enslow Publishers, Inc.

44 Fadem Road   PO Box 38
Box 699   Aldershot
Springfield, NJ 07081   Hants GU12 6BP
USA   UK

http://www.enslow.com

Library of Congress Cataloging-in-Publication Data

Lyman, Darryl, 1944–
    Holocaust rescuers: Ten stories of courage / Darryl Lyman
        p. cm. — (Collective biographies)
    Includes bibliographical references and index
    Summary: Discusses the efforts of ten individuals who did what
they could to save Jews from the Nazis, including Anna Borkowska,
Varian Fry, Irene Gut Opdyke, Mustafa Hardaga, Jørgen Kieler, Oskar
Schindler, Andrew Sheptitsky, Sempo Sugihara, Marion van Binsbergen
Pritchard, and Raoul Wallenberg.
    ISBN 0-7660-1114-3
    1. Righteous Gentiles in the Holocaust—Biography—Juvenile
literature. 2. World War, 1939–1945—Jews—Rescue—Juvenile
literature. [1. Righteous Gentiles in the Holocaust. 2. World
War, 1939–1945—Jews—Rescue.] I. Title. II. Series.
D804.65.L96 1999
362.87'81'0922—dc21
    [B]   98-21584
                                                    CIP
                                                     AC

Printed in the United States of America

10 9 8 7 6 5 4 3 2 1

To Our Readers:
All Internet addresses in this book were active and appropriate when we went to press.
Any comments or suggestions can be sent by e-mail to Comments@enslow.com or to
the address on the back cover.

Illustration Credits: Courtesy of Jørgen Kieler, pp. 54, 61; Courtesy of Patriarchate
magazine, pp. 74, 78; Courtesy of the USHMM Photo Archives, pp. 15, 18, 104,
110; Gay Block, courtesy of the USHMM Photo Archives, pp. 36, 41; Hiroki
Sugihara, courtesy of the USHMM Photo Archives, p. 86; Marion Pritchard, courtesy
of the USHMM Photo Archives, pp. 94, 100; Moreshet Archives, courtesy of the
USHMM Photo Archives, p. 22; National Archives, Washington, DC, courtesy of the
USHMM Photo Archives, p. 12; Photographic Archives, The Museum of Modern
Art, New York, pp. 24, 32; Professor Leopold Pfefferberg-Page, courtesy of the
USHMM Photo Archives, pp. 64, 68; Yad Vashem Photo Archives, courtesy of the
USHMM Photo Archives, pp. 46, 48, 82.

Cover Illustration: Courtesy of the USHMM Photo Archives

Contents

Introduction

The Holocaust was the persecution and mass murder of European Jews and others by Nazi Germany from 1939 to 1945. About 6 million Jews were killed—two thirds of all the Jews in Europe. Another 5 million people—Gypsies, homosexuals, the disabled, and others—were also killed.

Why did the Nazis hate, persecute, and eventually slaughter the Jews? Why did most ordinary citizens in Europe make no effort to stop the Nazis or to help the Jewish people? The answer is that the seeds of anti-Semitism (discrimination against Jews) and Nazism were planted in European culture at the very dawn of the Christian era. The Jews, as a people, were blamed for the crucifixion of Jesus. In the Middle Ages, church and state worked together to deny Jews citizenship and civil rights, to force them into ghettos (certain districts within cities), and to make them wear special clothing or badges identifying them as Jews.

Many people believed (incorrectly) that Jews murdered Christians, especially children, and used the victims' blood to make unleavened bread for the Passover religious ceremony. This belief is called the blood libel. For centuries Christians used the blood libel as an excuse to attack, arrest, and execute Jews.

Another false accusation against Jews was that they caused the Black Death of 1347–1351. The Black Death was a widespread outbreak of bubonic and pneumonic plague. Between one fourth and one third of Europe's population, perhaps 25 million people, died of the disease. Many people believed that Jews created the plague by poisoning food and water supplies to kill Christians. One reason Jews were blamed was that their religious practices of cleanliness sometimes protected them from diseases. However, in most cases, Jews drank from the same wells as their Christian neighbors and suffered similar losses from plague. In Vienna, Austria, for example, so many Jews died of the plague that the Jewish cemetery had to be enlarged. The main reason for blaming Jews was simple prejudice against them. Christians burned thousands of Jews at the stake for supposedly causing the Black Death.

Jews were allowed very few ways to earn their livings, mainly buying and selling on a small scale. But because Christians believed that lending money and charging interest (a practice called usury) was a sin, they also gave that job to Jews. Eventually, those in power used Jewish moneylenders to collect taxes so that the people's anger would be directed at the Jews and not at the Christian rulers. Jews thus became popularly associated with money and finance. This association was the origin of the false beliefs that "all Jews are rich" and "Jews control all the money."[1]

For centuries Jewish communities faced periodic raids that left homes destroyed and people massacred. Jews were often expelled from regions or countries.

During the 1700s in Europe, persecution of Jews eased due to the Enlightenment. During the Enlightenment—also called the Age of Reason—traditional social, religious, and political beliefs were rejected in favor of ideas based on reason. Philosophers who created these new ideas hoped to free people from old prejudices and from overly powerful authorities, such as the church and the government. One result of this general pursuit of freedom was that many Jews were given citizenship and civil rights. However, as Jews began to succeed in various walks of life, popular resentment of them increased.

During the 1800s, in Germany and elsewhere in Europe, anti-Semitism became a "science." Many books were published on the topic. A new theory developed: Jews were to be despised not for their religion but for their race. Jews were regarded as the slave race, while the Aryans (that is, the non-Jewish Germanic people) were considered the master race. Even Jews who had converted to Christianity and had become fully assimilated (absorbed) into European culture were condemned because of their "blood."

By the late 1800s many prominent politicians and philosophers in Germany and nearby Austria had accepted these anti-Semitic beliefs. The philosopher

Karl Eugen Dühring urged Germans to "exterminate such parasitic races as we exterminate snakes and beasts of prey."[2]

In 1889 Adolf Hitler was born in Austria, where he was exposed to anti-Semitism in various forms as he grew up. In 1913 he moved to Germany, and during World War I he served in the German Army. In 1920 he began to lead the National Socialist German Workers' party (Nazi party, for short). In 1925 Hitler published *Mein Kampf* ("My Struggle"), a book in which he clearly stated his intention to destroy all the Jews. He blamed the Jews for Germany's problems, including the loss of World War I and the resulting economic troubles. In laying this blame, he was following a centuries-old European tradition going back to the times when Jews were blamed for killing Jesus, bringing plague, and controlling money.

In January 1933 Hitler was appointed chancellor (prime minister) of Germany. He soon established a dictatorship. Between 1933 and 1935 the Nazi government, under Hitler's leadership, gradually took away Jews' rights through a series of laws. At first Jews were forced out of public life, such as the civil service, the government, and the professions (including law and education). Eventually, Jews lost citizenship and all legal rights. So when they were attacked by street thugs or Hitler's own secret police, Jews could not turn to the law or the courts for help.

The Nazis hoped that their laws would drive Jews out of Germany. But most Jews refused to leave. They believed that Hitler's rule would quickly end.

However, the Jewish condition became more desperate after November 9, 1938. Starting that night and continuing for about forty-eight hours, Nazis went on an anti-Jewish rampage throughout Germany. They destroyed more than 175 synagogues, looted and burned about seventy-five hundred Jewish-owned businesses, and killed nearly one hundred Jews. Up to thirty thousand Jews were arrested and forced to emigrate from Germany, leaving their money and property behind. The event has come to be called *Kristallnacht* ("Crystal Night"), known in English as the Night of Broken Glass. From this night on, the physical persecution of Jews became more open and violent.

Soon the Nazis extended their persecution to Jews in other countries as well. World War II began in 1939 when Germany invaded Poland. Over the next few years Germany conquered or began to dominate nearly all of Europe, including Belgium, Denmark, France, the Netherlands, Norway, and the western regions of the Soviet Union. Nazis herded millions of Jews throughout Europe into ghettos and then into concentration camps. Many Jews died from disease, starvation, and slave labor. Others were shot in mass executions. By 1942 the Nazis were ready to begin the program they called the Final Solution of the Jewish Question. The Final Solution

Germans pass by the broken shop window of a Jewish-owned business that was destroyed during *Kristallnacht.*

was to kill all the remaining Jews, mainly by poisoning them with gas in special death camps. By 1945, when Germany lost World War II, the Nazis had killed about 6 million Jews—men, women, and children.

The Jews were not alone as victims during the Holocaust. The Nazis also committed mass murder against other groups, including Gypsies, Poles, Slavs, Jehovah's Witnesses, the disabled, and homosexuals. About 5 million people in these other groups were killed.

Hitler was the guiding force behind the Holocaust. But many people willingly helped him. In Germany a large Nazi bureaucracy put his ideas into motion. Among the leaders were Adolf Eichmann, who helped to guide the Final Solution, and Heinrich Himmler, head of the SS (*Schutzstaffel*, special Nazi military police). Hitler could count on his most brutal orders being carried out by the SS and the Gestapo (secret police). He also enjoyed popular support from the masses. Most people did not know the details of Hitler's Final Solution. But they shared his anti-Semitism and said little when Jews began to disappear. Outside Germany, local populations often volunteered to help the German Nazis in murdering Jews. Hungarians, Lithuanians, Ukrainians, and others offered such help.

Many Jews tried to defend themselves. In ghettos, concentration camps, and even death camps, they took up arms and fought back. But the Nazi military strength was too great.

Gentiles (non-Jews) who hid Jews or helped them to escape faced torture or death at the hands of the Nazis. Nevertheless, some Gentiles risked their careers, their freedom, and their lives to assist Jews during this time.

The rescuers were men, women, and children who reacted by instinct to do the right thing. They simply could not turn their backs on innocent people whose lives were at stake. The rescuers came from many different backgrounds and countries. Even some German army officers risked their lives to protect Jews. Sometimes the rescuer was a whole town (like Le Chambon-sur-Lignon, France) or even a whole nation (notably Denmark, which evacuated its Jews to the safety of Sweden in 1943). The aid, too, varied: a job, a document, a hiding place, a bit of food, an article of clothing, or an escort to a border where freedom awaited. This book tells the stories of a cross section of those rescuers.

In 1953 Israel created a memorial to the victims of the Holocaust. It is located in Jerusalem and is called Yad Vashem. The name is Hebrew for "A Monument and a Name" or "Memorial and Record." In English, Yad Vashem is known as the Holocaust Martyrs' and Heroes' Remembrance Authority. Yad Vashem has honored the rescuers with various forms of recognition. The formal Hebrew title given to the rescuers is *Hasidei Ummot Ha-Olam*

The entire nation of Denmark joined the effort to ferry Jews to safety in Sweden.

("Righteous Ones Among the Nations of the World"), a phrase drawn from the Talmud, the Jewish holy book. In English the title is often shortened to "Righteous Gentiles" or simply "the Righteous." The highest form of tribute is a medallion bearing an inscription (in Hebrew) from the Mishnah (the basic part of the Talmud): "Whoever saves a single soul, it is as if he had saved the whole world."

Anna Borkowska

"Mother" of the Jews

As the mother superior of a Catholic convent near Vilna, Lithuania, Anna Borkowska witnessed the Nazi massacre of sixty thousand Jews in less than four months' time in 1941. Sickened by the slaughter, she resolved to help the Jews by hiding as many of them as she could and by smuggling weapons into the Vilna ghetto. The grateful Jews called her *Imma*, Hebrew for "Mother."[1]

When World War II began in 1939, Jews made up over one fourth of Vilna's two hundred thousand people. The Vilna Jews were used to anti-Semitism. They endured it from the local Lithuanians during 1920–1939, when Poland ruled the city. From 1939 to 1941, the Soviet Union controlled Vilna (which the

Anna Borkowska

Russians called Vilnius) and outlawed all Jewish organizations and activities there.

Conditions for Jews in Vilna grew even worse in June 1941 when the German army invaded the city. Helped by Lithuanian volunteers, the Germans soon rounded up thousands of Jews from Vilna and nearby districts. The Nazis took the Jews to Ponary, a wooded area six or seven miles from Vilna, and cold-bloodedly shot them to death. The remaining Jews were herded into a ghetto and killed in stages.

Anna Borkowska was about forty years old during this troubled time. Polish by birth, she had graduated from Krakow University as a science major and become a Catholic holy sister. By the fateful year of 1941, she headed a group of seven or eight nuns at a small convent in Kolonia Wilenska, three miles outside Vilna.

Borkowska agreed to conceal Jews in her convent. The number of men, women, and children who found refuge with her varied at different times, but there were often more visitors than nuns.

She remembered one of them as Mrs. K, who arrived one October night at the convent during a Nazi killing frenzy. "On a small sledge I brought little Sala, Mrs. K's granddaughter," Borkowska later wrote. The four-year-old girl was serious and quiet. "But once, when there was a noise in the courtyard, the little one asked gravely, 'Granny, must we go now to Ponary?' She perished in Ponary, with her grandmother."[2]

Many of the young Jewish men and women wanted to resist the Nazis by taking up arms. At first Borkowska tried to convince them to concentrate on saving people rather than using guns. When the Jews finally persuaded her that they had to fight, she personally went out to find ways of acquiring weapons.

Her convent served as a meeting place for Jewish ghetto leaders. One of those leaders, Abba Kovner, who later became a famous Hebrew poet, organized a Jewish rebellion in Vilna from a cellar in the convent.[3] There he composed the first declaration of the Jews' uprising against the Nazis. The declaration was secretly printed in the convent and distributed in the ghetto on January 1, 1942. "Let's not allow ourselves," Kovner wrote, "to be led like sheep to the slaughter."[4] His efforts led to the formation of the United Partisans Organization, the first known Jewish resistance group in the Holocaust.

When Jewish fighters returned to the Vilna ghetto, Borkowska guarded the arms they had stored in the convent. She also supplied other weapons that she somehow obtained. One day she went to the ghetto with four hand grenades. As she passed them to Kovner, she whispered, "God is with you, my dear one."[5] Kovner was unfamiliar with the grenades, so the mother superior, a former science student, instructed him in their proper use.

Borkowska called the Jewish fighters "my boys and girls."[6] Abba Kovner, disguised as a female novice (beginner at the convent), stayed with her for weeks. Another was Chaika Grossman, who later became a member of the Israeli Knesset (parliament). Arieh Wilner was her favorite because "each of us wanted to be able to look into the other's soul," she later wrote. "We had respect for each other's convictions. We exchanged our philosophies, not without some sort of influence on each other. In our discussions we tried to escape from the monstrous reality into the world of ideas."[7]

One day in 1943, word arrived that her boys and girls were leaving Vilna to go to Warsaw, Poland. After nearly half a million Jews had been sent from the Warsaw ghetto to death camps, the last sixty thousand decided to resist. Other Jews, including Borkowska's friends, went there to help. "I bade them farewell with a heavy heart," she later remembered. "I knew what was in store for them."[8] When she visited them in Vilna before they left, she went in ordinary clothing, not her nun's habit, which would have attracted the Nazis' attention to the Jews. During April and May of 1943, the Jews in Warsaw fought courageously, but most of them were captured or killed. The ghetto itself was demolished.

Many of Borkowska's boys and girls sacrificed their lives at Warsaw. Arieh Wilner died there. When she later wrote about this sad episode, she identified some of her friends affectionately by their first names only. A boy she called Israel suffered in Warsaw and then perished in a concentration camp. Her girl Tauba was gentle, but she was courageous enough to

Borkowska (center) attends a Yad Vashem award ceremony in 1984, where she was honored as one of the Righteous Among the Nations of the World. Abba Kovner, one of the Jews she rescued, stands on the right.

throw a grenade under a German car before being killed. Sarenka, who had bravely faced the death of her husband and the separation from her child, lost her life in Warsaw. Borkowska grieved for them all.

The Germans grew increasingly suspicious that Borkowska was helping Jews. In September 1943 they had her and one of her nuns arrested.[9] The mother superior was questioned and released while the other nun was sent to a forced-labor camp. Soon afterward the church authorities closed the Kolonia Wilenska convent and separated the sisters, ordering them to different locations.

After the war Borkowska resigned from her duties with the Catholic church. In her later years she lived on a pension in Warsaw. She died in 1988.

Yad Vashem honored her as a Righteous Gentile in 1984. On that occasion, Abba Kovner, speaking for those rescued by Anna Borkowska, called her "a source of inspiration. For all who wandered in that desert of animosity, she was with them at the time the angels mourned."[10]

Varian Fry

Varian Fry

Assignment: Rescue

As the representative of a private American rescue organization, Varian Fry led a small group that helped about two thousand Jewish and non-Jewish refugees to escape from Nazi-occupied France in 1940–1941. The arrival in the United States of the escapees had a major impact on American culture because many of them were leading artists, writers, musicians, scientists, and politicians.[1]

Varian M. Fry was born in New York City in 1908. He became a classicist (a scholar of the ancient Greek and Roman world), earning a bachelor's degree at Harvard College and taking graduate courses at Columbia University. He also developed an interest in modern foreign affairs. By 1940 he was working as an editor at the Foreign Policy

Association, which published books on political and economic issues.

Fry kept a close watch on events in Europe. Because of Hitler's social, cultural, and political persecution in Germany and eastern Europe, many anti-Nazis fled to France. A large number of refugees settled in the northern city of Paris, the capital. When France fell to Germany in June 1940, the two countries signed an agreement that divided France into two zones. The Germans occupied the northern section; the French established a Nazi-influenced government in the south, centered in Vichy and headed by Marshal Henri-Philippe Pétain. Thousands of French, German, and other European refugees, both Jews and non-Jews, fled south toward the port city of Marseilles, where they hoped to leave the country by boat. But the Vichy government closed the borders and trapped the refugees in France. They lived in constant fear because the Franco-German agreement had a "surrender on demand" clause, which meant that the Vichy French had to hand over fugitives, both German and non-German, whenever the Nazis demanded them. The refugees knew that in Nazi hands they would face prison, torture, and almost certain death.

The "surrender on demand" clause angered many people in the United States. A group in New York City founded the Emergency Rescue Committee. The committee's purpose was to send to Marseilles a representative who would help leading cultural figures to leave France before the Nazis could arrest them. The representative would work openly and legally if possible, but secretly and illegally if necessary, to save lives. The organization had no connection with the American government, which was not yet in the war. But one of the committee's sponsors was Eleanor Roosevelt. She convinced her husband, President Franklin D. Roosevelt, to grant special visas (written approvals for passing into or out of a country) to the refugees so that they could enter the United States.[2]

Varian Fry volunteered to go to France for the Emergency Rescue Committee. He had a deep appreciation for the intellectual and cultural achievements of many of the refugees. "I knew that among those trapped in France were many writers, artists, and musicians whose work had given me much pleasure," he later explained.

> I didn't know them personally, but I felt a deep love for these people and a gratitude for the many hours of happiness their books and pictures and music had given me. Now they were in danger. It was my duty to help them, just as they—without knowing it—had helped me in the past.[3]

He also had a personal reason for wanting to do the rescue operation. During a visit to Berlin in 1935, "I saw young Nazi toughs smash up Jewish-owned shops," he later reported.

> I watched in horror as they dragged people out into the streets and beat and kicked them. I

watched as they drove men and women, cut and bleeding down the streets, hitting them with clubs, calling them vile names. They knocked down an elderly man and, as he lay on the pavement, the young toughs kicked him in the face again and again.[4]

He also witnessed a gang of Nazis brutalizing a Jew in a restaurant. They shoved a knife through the man's hand, pinning it to the table.[5] Fry had seen what evil the Nazis were capable of, and he wanted to rescue as many people as possible from the tormentors' clutches.

"Friends warned me of the danger," he later wrote. "They said I was a fool to go. I, too, could be walking into a trap. I might never come back alive."[6]

Fry arrived in Marseilles in August 1940 with three thousand dollars strapped to his leg and lists of refugees in his pocket. He soon realized that he would get no official help. To please the Germans, French authorities refused to grant exit visas to the fugitives, who therefore could not legally leave France. American officials in France, eager to maintain friendly relations with the Vichy government, would not help Fry break French laws. To fulfill his mission, Fry had to sneak the refugees out of France.

He set up two operations. One was open and legal. He brought to France a letter from the International Young Men's Christian Association (YMCA). The YMCA stated that Fry was its representative. It also said that Fry was helping refugees to obtain overseas visas and giving the people money to live on while they waited. That information was true, and the work was legal. But it was a cover for his second operation—secretly and illegally smuggling men and women out of the country.

Fry assembled a group of about ten persons to help him. He began with Albert O. Hirschman (nicknamed Beamish because of his grin). Hirschman was a German refugee who became the group's specialist on illegal matters, such as exchanging money on the black market and obtaining false identity cards. During the day, refugees poured into Fry's hotel room (which he used as a temporary office) to seek help. At night, he and his staff held meetings in his bathroom, running water to cover the sounds of their voices.[7]

The hardest part of Fry's job was deciding if an applicant was a real refugee or an undercover agent. He decided "to give each refugee the full benefit of the doubt. Otherwise we might refuse help to someone who was really in danger and learn later that he had been dragged away to Dachau or Buchenwald [Nazi concentration camps in Germany] because we had turned him down."[8] However, each person was asked to provide references.

To get people out of France, Fry and his assistants developed escape routes to the border between France and Spain. The rescuers constantly had to change the routes as old ones were discovered. Fry himself often accompanied refugees to the border. A refugee couple, Johannes and Lisa Fitto, helped him to organize one of the most successful routes. It was called the F Route, a rugged mountain climb into Spain.

From Spain the refugees went to Portugal, where they boarded boats headed for the United States. They carried legitimate United States entry visas supplied by Fry. However, other necessary documents were usually forged, such as French exit visas and Spanish transit visas. Fry's assistants also managed to give some refugees illegal passports (documents issued by a country to identify citizens who may be traveling abroad) from such countries as Lithuania, Panama, and even China. Sometimes the fugitives wore disguises.

In the autumn of 1940, Fry moved his operations out of the hotel and opened an office. He called his organization the American Rescue Center, a legal relief committee that covered his secret activities. Only a few of his employees knew of his real mission.

French and American authorities, however, suspected that he was engaged in underground work. They constantly watched and questioned him. Several times the French police raided and searched his home and office. Each time, Fry quickly destroyed secret documents (false visas, passports, and so on) before the police could find them. United States officials in France, still wanting to maintain friendly relations with the Vichy government, tried to restrict his movements and urged him to go back to America.

To escape the tension of their work, Fry and some of his assistants rented a quiet estate, the Villa Air-Bel, on the edge of Marseilles. But the quiet was short-lived. In December 1940 Marshal Pétain visited Marseilles. Just before he arrived, local police arrested about twenty thousand people, including the occupants of the villa. Fry and his group were held for several days on a prison ship in the Marseilles harbor before the police released them. The only reason given to Fry for the arrests was that the police were looking for Communists. However, the real reason for the arrests was probably to ensure Pétain's safety from people who had disagreements with the Vichy government. After Fry was released, both French and American authorities increased their observation of him and his committee, hoping to get enough evidence to deport him to the United States.[9]

By January 1941 American officials in France were desperate to get rid of Fry. They took away his passport and refused to return it till he was ready to leave the country. For the next seven months he continued his work without a passport. That summer the chief of police at Marseilles warned him that he would soon be arrested. When Fry asked why, the chief replied, "Because you have helped and protected Jews and anti-Nazis."[10]

From left: André Breton, Jacqueline Breton, Max Ernst, and Varian Fry (seated) in the offices of the Centre Americain de Secours, Marseilles, 1941.

Finally, in late August 1941, he was arrested and led to the Spanish border by French police. But because he had no exit and transit visas, he was not immediately allowed to enter Spain. Several days later, in early September, Fry boarded a train and left France.

"I have to admit," Fry wrote to his mother as he crossed into Spain, "that I am proud to have stayed. I stayed because the refugees needed me. But it took courage, and courage is a quality I hadn't previously been sure I possessed."[11]

Fry was frustrated that he could not stay in France to help more refugees. But while he was there, he delivered many important people to freedom. "Some of them, of course, are now a part of the scientific and cultural history of our time," he observed.[12] As leaders in their fields, they embodied the highest intellectual achievements and cultural values in Europe. After they immigrated to the United States, some stayed only till the end of the war and others remained for the rest of their lives. While in the United States, they dramatically enriched American culture.

Many of the refugees rescued by Fry were Jews. Hannah Arendt, for example, was a philosopher and political scientist whose studies revealed much about the origins of twentieth-century dictatorships. Marc Chagall, more than any other artist of his time, kept alive the spirit of emotion and poetry in art. Jacques-Salomon Hadamard, a pioneer in modern mathematics, was known as the Einstein of France. Wanda Landowska led the twentieth-century revival of the harpsichord. Jacques Lipchitz was one of the world's greatest modern sculptors. Otto Meyerhof won a Nobel Prize in 1922 for his discoveries about chemical reactions that occur when muscles are working. Meyerhof's greatest contribution in the United States was his teaching at the University of Pennsylvania from 1940 to 1951. Franz Werfel began his career as a modern German poet. But in America he became famous for his popular novels, such as *The Song of Bernadette* (1941).

Among the non-Jews rescued by Fry was the novelist Heinrich Mann, brother of the great German writer Thomas Mann. Another was Alfredo Mendizabel, Spain's leading Catholic philosopher.

When he returned to the United States, Fry wrote *Surrender on Demand* (1945), a book about his experiences rescuing refugees in Vichy France. He also served as editor of the *Living Age* and *Common Sense* magazines and assistant editor of the *New Republic*. Other important jobs he held were executive director of the American Labor Conference on International Affairs and president of Cinemark, Inc., which made commercial movies for television. Fry was active in the American Civil Liberties Union, the International League for the Rights of Man, the American China Policy Association, and the American Film Council. Near the end of his life, he returned to his first love: the classics. At the time of his death in Easton, Connecticut, on September 13, 1967, he was a teacher of Latin at Joel Barlow High School in Redding, Connecticut.

He left behind his second wife, Annette T. Riley. His first wife, Eileen A. Hughes, had died. Fry had three children.[13]

The year after his death, a new edition of his book was published. It was titled *Assignment: Rescue.*

"Varian Fry is certainly one of the great men of this century," said Willi Spira ("Bill Freier"), a cartoonist who helped Fry by forging documents. "America can be proud of him."[14] Israel honored him as the first American on its list of Righteous Ones Among the Nations of the World.

Irene Gut Opdyke

3

Irene Gut Opdyke

Jews Under the Gazebo

While some rescuers of Jews during the Holocaust held positions of authority and prestige in society, many others came from more humble backgrounds. One of the latter was the housekeeper Irene Gut (later Opdyke), who hid a dozen Jews in a secret chamber under the garden at a villa in Tarnopol, Poland, where she worked for a Nazi major.

Before World War II, Poland had a large Jewish community of 3.3 million people, which was nearly 10 percent of the Polish population. Polish Jews had long suffered anti-Semitism. The Polish government would not allow Jews to establish their own social, religious, and educational institutions. Economic discrimination forced the majority of Polish Jews into poverty. And from 1919 to 1939, many Jews were killed in pogroms (organized massacres).

Irene Gut was born in Poland in 1921.[1] Many experiences in her youth contributed to her becoming a rescuer. As a youngster she played with Jewish children, learning that there was no difference between them and herself. In her early teens she was bedridden for months with tuberculosis, learning what it felt like to need help. She saw her mother, a devout Catholic, put out a helping hand to others by cooking food for poor neighbors, offering shelter and nursing care to Gypsies, and regularly visiting the sick daughter of a nearby Jewish family. Irene, the eldest of five daughters, did her part by taking care of her little sisters.

She enjoyed caregiving so much that she decided to become a nurse. On September 1, 1939, while she was attending a nursing school in the Polish city of Radom, the German army invaded Poland from the west. With some other nurses, she worked with the Polish Army to resist the Germans. However, on September 17 Poland was invaded from the east by the Soviets. On September 19 the Germans and the Soviets met near Brest Litovsk, and on September 28 Germany and the Soviet Union divided Poland.

A band of Soviet soldiers caught, raped, and beat Gut, and then left her for dead in a forest. She was found and taken to a Russian hospital. After she recovered she worked as a nurse in a prisoner-of-war camp. In 1941 she returned to Poland in an exchange of prisoners between the Soviets and the Germans, who controlled her home territory of Radom.

After a brief reunion with her parents, Gut was forced to work in a German munitions factory. One day the fumes at the factory overcame her and she fainted at the feet of a German major, Eduard Ruegemer. When she awoke, Ruegemer recruited her to serve meals to German officers at their club, formerly the town's hotel.

While working there one day, she heard nearby gunfire and screams. Rushing to the window, she opened the curtain and witnessed men, women, and children being shot to death behind the building. Ruegemer told her to ignore the sight, it was simply the extermination of "vermin" in the ghetto.[2] Each day after that incident, she and one of her sisters, also a waitress there, secretly took leftover food from the officers' club to the Jews in the ghetto.

On another occasion Gut and her sister saw Nazis use machine guns to shoot Jews down into open graves. "I asked God to give me responsibility, to bring me the opportunity to help," Gut later said, "even if my own life should be taken."[3]

One day the Jews were marched from the ghetto out of town. Gut watched as weakened, pregnant, wounded, and crippled people tried to keep up with the others. A Nazi guard tore a crying infant from its mother's arms and slammed it head first against the ground. "I never forget that young woman's scream as she leaped to save her child," Gut later recalled.

"With one bullet to the head, she was dead, lying next to her child."[4]

When Major Ruegemer was assigned to head an ammunition factory near the Russian border at Tarnopol, he took Gut with him. On the way, they passed through the Polish city of Lwow. There she witnessed Nazi soldiers beating a rabbi to death and saw a baby tossed into the air "and shot like a bird."[5] The factory at Tarnopol was operated with the forced labor of three hundred Jews from the nearby ghetto. The ghetto also supplied twelve Jews to help Gut as she supervised the laundry service where the major lived.

She became close friends with her Jewish helpers. Once she managed to obtain a pass for one of them to visit her parents in the ghetto. While the woman was there, however, the ghetto was raided, and she did not return on time. Gut went to the ghetto and rescued the frightened woman from the rubble.

Whenever she could, Gut listened to the Nazis' mealtime talk and passed along the information to her laundry helpers, who in turn sent the news to the ghetto. These advance warnings enabled the ghetto dwellers to prepare for Nazi raids by hiding or escaping into the forest. Gut saved many lives through these warnings.

One day in July 1943, Gut overheard the Nazis planning to wipe out the whole ghetto once and for all. When she passed along this information, her Jewish friends asked her for help. She was frantic.

Gut Opdyke (second from right) poses with Jews who worked in a Gestapo laundry. As a housekeeper for a German major in Tarnopol, she used his villa to hide Jews.

How could she hide her twelve helpers? A few days before the scheduled killing of the Jews, the major received word that he would be moving into a villa. He asked Gut to go with him as his housekeeper. When she saw the villa, she decided to hide the Jews there.

Before the major moved into his new home, Gut stole his keys while he was asleep and let the Jews into the villa. At first she had to juggle her friends. When the major was downstairs, she hid the Jews in the attic; when he was upstairs, she hid them in the cellar.

Then Gut learned that the architect of the villa had guessed about the coming persecution of the Jews and had built a secret hiding place under the gazebo in the garden. She immediately put the Jews there. Sometimes she had to divert the attention of people who went to the garden. Once, for example, a Nazi officer took his girlfriend to the gazebo. One of the Jews had a cold and was coughing. Gut, fearing that the Nazi would hear the coughing below him, interrupted the lovers by offering them food and drink. The angry officer took his lady elsewhere.

Another problem was that one of the women under the gazebo was pregnant. A baby would mean noise—lots of it. The woman offered to abort the baby to maintain the safety of the other people hiding with her, but Gut was against the abortion. "I saw so many babies killed," she told the woman. "Please don't do it. You'll see—you'll be free by the time you have to give birth. You will be liberated."[6] The woman decided to wait.

While shopping in town one day in September 1943, Gut was forced to witness the public hanging of a Polish family and a Jewish family. The former were punished for having hidden the latter. The execution was a warning to others who might hide Jews. Terrified, Gut rushed home. Upset at what she had just seen, she forgot her usual practice of locking the kitchen door when her friends were there to prepare food for the others. The major walked into the kitchen and caught her with several of the Jews. He was furious. She pleaded with him for mercy. After a few hours he finally agreed to let the Jews stay—for a price. Gut would have to become his lover. "He was in love—an old man in love with a pretty woman," Gut later explained. "It was a small price to pay for the many lives."[7]

Eventually, the major grew to enjoy the Jews' cooking. He called them by their first names, and they called him Grandpa.

In February 1944, after the Jews had been under the gazebo for eight months, the Soviet army advanced into the region. The Germans, including Major Ruegemer, evacuated.

The Jews fled into the forest. Gut went with them, refusing to go with the Germans. Soon the Soviets came and liberated the area. On May 4, 1944, the pregnant woman finally gave birth in freedom. "That was my payment for whatever hell I went through—seeing that little boy," Gut later said.[8]

After the war ended in 1945, Gut went to a Jewish refugee camp in Germany. Homeless people in this camp were helped to settle in other countries. An American named William Opdyke interviewed her in preparation for her immigration to the United States. In 1949 she arrived in America. In 1955 she married William Opdyke. They had one daughter.

Irene Gut Opdyke moved with her husband and daughter to California, where she worked for many years as an interior decorator. She seldom spoke about her experiences in World War II. In the 1970s, however, she heard about neo-Nazis who claimed that the Holocaust was a hoax. Infuriated, she began to devote herself to giving lectures all over the United States, telling people the truth about what the Nazis did to the Jews.

Her favorite audiences are children. "You can do what I did! Right now!" she tells them. "Stand up when you hear name-calling, when you see skin-heads. You are the future of the nation."[9] Her message to adults is similar: "You have to give not just money, but you must give of yourself."[10]

4

Mustafa Hardaga
Muslim Rescuer

When the German army invaded Yugoslavia in 1941, Mustafa Hardaga sheltered a Jewish family; he later arranged for their escape to safety. Hardaga, his wife, Zayneba, and his father-in-law, Ahmed Sadik, were the first three Muslims honored by Israel for helping Jews during World War II.[1]

When war broke out in 1939, Yugoslavia was neutral. But on March 25, 1941, under the leadership of Prince Paul, the nation joined the Axis headed by Nazi Germany. The next day Paul was overthrown and a new, anti-German government took over. Angry at the loss of his new ally, Hitler called for the invasion of Yugoslavia. On April 6, Germany attacked Yugoslavia, which surrendered on April 17.

Mustafa Hardaga (then deceased), Zayneba Hardaga (fourth from right), and Ahmed Sadik (not pictured) became the first Muslims to be named Righteous Gentiles. On June 16, 1985, they were honored with a tree-planting ceremony. Yosef Kabilio (second from right), a Jew they worked to save, attended the ceremony.

Mustafa Hardaga was a merchant who owned property all over the city of Sarajevo, the capital of the Yugoslavian republic of Bosnia (now part of the independent nation of Bosnia and Herzegovina). On one of his tracts of land was a factory owned by a Jew, his friend Yosef Kabilio.

When the Germans bombed Sarajevo in April 1941, they destroyed the apartment building where Kabilio and his wife and two children lived. Hardaga insisted that the Kabilios move into his own house.

Soon the Nazis marched into Sarajevo. About one third of the people in the city were Muslims, many of whom shared the Nazis' anti-Semitism. Supported by the invaders, Muslims and other anti-Semites went on a rampage against the Jews. The rioters attacked Jews and destroyed much of their property, including a synagogue.

In September the Nazis, helped by the local police, began to deport the city's ten thousand Jews (about one tenth of the city's population) to concentration camps that the Nazis had set up in Yugoslavia. The first groups of Jews were sent to Kruscica. From there, the women and children went to Loborgrad, while the men were shipped to Jasenovac, where they were killed. Soon women and children, too, were sent to their deaths at Jasenovac. By early 1942 the Jewish population of Sarajevo was nearly gone, most to concentration camps, some to safety abroad.

Mustafa Hardaga's wife, Zayneba

During this time the Gestapo set up headquarters across the street from Mustafa Hardaga's house and posted signs threatening death to anyone who hid Jews. At night the people in Hardaga's house could hear the screams of prisoners being tortured by the Gestapo.

Despite danger from the Nazis and pressure from within the Muslim community, Mustafa and Zayneba Hardaga continued to hide the Kabilios. Both families witnessed the anti-Semitic riots. "These deeds," Kabilio later said, "only strengthened the Hardagas' feelings of friendship towards us and their sympathy for what was happening to the Jews."[2]

Kabilio knew that the only way to save his family was to get them out of Sarajevo. Their best hope was to escape to the Italian-controlled zone of Yugoslavia. Italy, along with Bulgaria and Hungary, had helped Germany to occupy Yugoslavia. The four invaders had then divided the conquered country. Italy took the area known as Dalmatia, along the Adriatic Sea, which separates Italy from Yugoslavia. In Italy and in all areas occupied by Italy, Jews were subject to harsh laws and restrictions. But the Italians repeatedly refused German demands to deport Jews from Italian zones to concentration camps.

Mustafa Hardaga helped to arrange the smuggling of Yosef Kabilio's wife and children out of Sarajevo and into the city of Mostar in the Italian-controlled zone.[3] The smuggling was carried out by a Serbian friend of Kabilio's. Kabilio himself, however, was too well known to go with them. The prominent businessman would have been recognized during the trip.

The Nazis transferred the operation of Kabilio's factory, which manufactured plumbing materials, to an ethnic German who had previously been Kabilio's chief accountant. The new boss accused Kabilio of trying to sabotage the factory to prevent the Nazis from using it. Now that the Nazis were looking specifically for him, Kabilio knew he had to find a new hiding place because the Hardagas lived too close to the factory.

Under cover of darkness, he sneaked into the local military hospital, where a friend, Captain Radovich, was in charge. The captain disguised Kabilio as a sick prisoner and hid him for two months.

One night, however, the police came and arrested him. He was locked up with other Jews in the local prison. Every morning the prisoners were chained together and taken out to shovel snow off the streets. One day Zayneba Hardaga saw Kabilio and the other prisoners walking back through the snow to their cells. She wept at the sight, and every day after that she took food to Kabilio and a few other prisoners.

After one month of imprisonment, Kabilio escaped, but he was soon recaptured. The Gestapo now sentenced him to death. With eight other condemned men, he was sent to Pale, about twenty miles from Sarajevo. The prisoners were forced to perform hard labor, repairing sabotaged water and sewage pipes. Starved, they resorted to eating grass and snails. Nazis commonly used this method of working and starving Jews to death.

Again the Hardagas reached out to help. The family sent food to Kabilio and the other prisoners. "The courage of the Hardaga family touched all of us," Kabilio later testified, "and gave us strength to keep living in our imprisonment."[4]

After the prisoners had been in Pale for two months, the guards received an order to execute the condemned men. However, before the execution could be carried out, a member of the Yugoslav Army, Captain Reinman, secretly released the nine prisoners. With civilian clothing that the Hardagas had smuggled to them, the prisoners slipped out after dark, each going his own way. Eight of the escapees were caught and shot to death.[5] Kabilio, however, survived by making it through the woods and back to the Hardaga family. "They were extremely happy to see me," he later wrote, "laughing and crying at the same time."[6] He learned that the Hardagas had been sending money to his family during his imprisonment.

The next morning Kabilio met Zayneba's father, Ahmed Sadik. Sadik himself had hidden the Papo family, Jewish friends of the Kabilios, and had arranged for them to reach the Italian zone. Shortly before the end of the war, Sadik was denounced for helping Jews and was killed in a concentration camp.

The Hardagas did everything they could to make Kabilio's stay in their house comfortable, even though their own safety was at stake. Posters on walls still warned that anyone caught sheltering Jews would be put to death. And every night the Hardaga household could still hear screams from people being tortured in the Gestapo headquarters across the street. "I feared that if I were to stay," Kabilio later remembered, "I might bring tragedy upon the Hardaga family."[7]

So Kabilio made the decision to leave the city. The danger of being recognized was now less than the risk of staying where he was. With Mustafa Hardaga's assistance, Kabilio arranged for an acquaintance to smuggle him out of Sarajevo and into the Italian zone, where he rejoined his family.

When the war ended in 1945, only 2,400 of Sarajevo's 10,000 Jews were still alive. Most had survived by fleeing, as the Kabilios had, to the Italian zone.

At the end of the war, the Hardagas welcomed the Kabilios back to Sarajevo. "The jewelry that we had left in their home," Kabilio noted, "was returned to us in the same box we had packed it in."[8]

In 1950 the Kabilios moved to the new Jewish state of Israel, settling in Jerusalem. On the strength of Kabilio's testimony, Israel, in a ceremony held on June 16, 1985, honored Mustafa Hardaga, by then deceased, along with his wife and her father. They were the first Muslims to be officially named

Righteous Gentiles for rescuing Jews during the Holocaust.

The president of the Sha'aria Islamic Court in Jerusalem, Subhi Abu-Ghosh, attended the ceremony. "All you did was part of the humane and religious values our Prophet Mohammed spoke of so often when he taught about the rights of neighbors," Abu-Ghosh said. "We Moslems in Israel are very proud of you."[9]

In 1994 Sarajevo was once again torn apart by war. This time the Muslims were the endangered group. Israel, in gratitude for the Hardagas' rescue of Jews during World War II, now rescued the Hardagas. The Israeli government removed Mustafa Hardaga's widow, Zayneba, and the rest of her family from Sarajevo and brought them safely to the Jewish homeland.

Jørgen Kieler

5

Jørgen Kieler

Danish Rescue by Boat

During the German occupation of Denmark in World War II, Jørgen Kieler was a young medical student actively involved with the resistance movement against the invaders. In the autumn of 1943, word spread that the Germans were going to round up all the Jews in Denmark. Kieler and other Danes quickly put together and carried out a remarkable plan to save the Danish Jews by sending them to Sweden on boats. The operation was so successful that all but a small percentage of Danish Jews escaped. Later Kieler was imprisoned and seriously injured under torture by the Nazis.

The German occupation of Denmark began on April 9, 1940, when German troops entered the country. The Germans, who regarded the Danes as racial "brothers," claimed that they wanted to protect Denmark from attack by Allied nations, such as England. The Germans said that they would not interfere with Denmark's internal affairs if the Danes promised not to resist. The Danish government quickly agreed.

However, in the autumn of 1942, Hitler changed his policy toward Denmark. To increase Germany's strength for the war effort, he decided to make Denmark part of Germany.

Jørgen Kieler, twenty-three years old at the time of the rescue operation in 1943, had resented the Germans ever since they occupied Denmark. Like many other Danes, he felt a deep sense of national shame at the country's quick surrender. Those upset at the Danish government's lack of official resistance to the Nazis decided to resist privately. Some resisted passively, without resorting to life-threatening aggressive action. Others, like Kieler, resisted actively, with violence when necessary.[1] Kieler belonged to one of many groups that engaged in strikes, riots, sabotage, and other acts against the German occupiers.

During this time, Kieler lived in a three-room apartment in the center of Copenhagen, the capital of Denmark, with his brother and two of his sisters. All the siblings had moved from a provincial town to the metropolis to pursue their studies. Their apartment became a meeting place for active resisters, including other students and naval cadets. In their rooms, the Kielers kept a printing press for making anti-Nazi literature. They also stored guns stolen from the Germans and from the Danish navy head-quarters.

The Germans became increasingly angry at the Danes' resistance. Finally, in August 1943 the German army took away the Danish army's weapons, forced the Danish government to resign, and imprisoned the country's leader, King Christian X. The Germans took over complete political control of the country.

According to Kieler, the Germans soon made two mistakes that galvanized the Danish people against them. First, in the middle of September, the Germans executed a Danish saboteur. Second, the invaders began to persecute the Jews. The Jews had previously been under the protection of the Danish government. Unlike many other European countries, Denmark did not have a strong tradition of anti-Semitism. In fact, Jews were well established and happy in Denmark. With Jewish lives now threatened, even passive resisters were ready to save them through strong action.[2]

In September 1943 Georg Duckwitz, a German naval attaché in Copenhagen, received secret instructions to prepare four cargo ships to carry away all Denmark's Jews on October 1. The Nazis planned to send the Jews to concentration camps in eastern Europe. Duckwitz was disgusted by Nazi terror tactics against Jews and others. While working in

Denmark, he developed close ties with Danish political leaders. On September 28 he told some of those leaders about the planned round-up of Danish Jews. On September 29 this news was given to Jews in synagogues, and from there the word spread throughout the Jewish community.

Soon the people of Denmark joined in a widespread effort to save the Jews by smuggling them out of the country on boats to the safety of nearby Sweden. During World War II Sweden was neutral. By 1943 Germany was anxious to avoid pushing Sweden into joining the Allies. Germany had recently suffered military defeats. For example, it lost in North Africa in 1942 and in the Soviet Union during the winter of 1942–1943. So when Sweden exercised its independence, Germany backed off. In July 1943 Sweden declared that German soldiers could no longer cross Swedish land, and Germany agreed. In Sweden, then, the Danish Jews would be safe from the Germans.

On its eastern border, Denmark is separated from Sweden by a narrow stretch of ocean called the Øresund. At one point, the Øresund is only two-and-a-half miles wide. Copenhagen lies on that border, so it was the natural place to gather most of the Danish Jews for the crossing to Sweden.

Jørgen Kieler, along with his brother and sisters, joined in the Danish national effort to save the Jews. Within the short span of forty-eight hours after learning of the Germans' intentions, the Danes raised enough money and found enough boats for the rescue operation. Kieler's group solicited money from refugees, from people living on wealthy estates surrounding Copenhagen, and from other private sources. The group organized a small fleet, which included fishing boats and a supply ship that made daily trips to a lighthouse in the middle of the Øresund.

Kieler's procedure was to find Jews, take them to the Copenhagen harbor, and protect them till they could actually board the boats and escape. His group rescued about fifteen hundred Jews without any loss of life.[3] He later used the same method to send spies, agents, weapons, and secret material from Denmark to Sweden.

Of Denmark's approximately eight thousand Jews, only about four hundred to six hundred were captured. They were sent to Theresienstadt, a town in Czechoslovakia. The Nazis used the town as a ghetto where Jews were kept till they could be transferred to death camps. Near the ghetto was a concentration camp for political prisoners, both Jews and non-Jews. Because of pressure by the Danish government, no Danish Jew was sent to a death camp. A small number died of disease at Theresienstadt.

Kieler believed that the Danish rescue mission succeeded for several reasons. Crucial at the very beginning was the early warning by Georg Duckwitz of the Nazis' intention to seize the Jews. Sweden's availability as a nearby refuge was, of course, absolutely necessary. Another helpful factor was the inability of the German navy to guard the entire length of Denmark's long coastline. Most important of all, though, the Danish people, risking the wrath of the Germans, made the decision to save the Jews. According to Kieler, the Danes did what they did because the active and passive resisters finally found common ground. The Danish people had a long tradition of concern for human welfare, and Denmark was virtually free of anti-Semitism.[4]

"National independence and democracy were our common goals," Kieler later wrote,

> but the persecution of the Jews added a new and overwhelming dimension to the fight against Hitler: human rights. Our responsibility toward and our respect for the individual human being became the primary goals of the struggle, a struggle which required a maximum of moral and physical strength from the rescuer and the rescued alike, and above all from those who were caught by the Germans.[5]

The Germans finally caught up with Kieler and his friends. After about four months of active resistance and twenty-five separate actions (some against the German war industry), Kieler's group was broken up by the invaders. Two of Kieler's associates were shot in action, two committed suicide, two were executed after being tortured, and two died in a concentration camp. The others were deported or

This photo was found after the war in the archives of the Gestapo. It was taken in the Frøslev prison camp in Denmark in September 1944 by German police before Kieler's deportation to the Neuengamme Concentration Camp.

went underground. Kieler himself was captured by the Germans. While interrogating him, they fractured his skull. Later he spent time in two concentration camps.[6]

Danish resistance, however, never stopped. The Danes continued to harass the Germans till the end of the war in 1945.

After the war, Kieler became a medical doctor. He has served as director of the Danish Cancer Research Institute and as president of the Freedom Foundation in Copenhagen.

For many years, Jewish groups have thanked and honored Jørgen Kieler and his friends for rescuing the Jews of Denmark. But Kieler maintains that the Danes, too, owe something to the Jews. The Danes were inspired by the Jews' situation to unify themselves at an important time in their national history. "Jews don't owe us gratitude," Kieler says; "rather, we owe each other mutual friendship."[7]

6

Oskar Schindler
Schindler's List

The Holocaust produced some unlikely rescuers—among them even a few Nazis. One of the most surprising was Oskar Schindler, an apparently self-centered businessman who loved to buy luxuries, drink liquor, and chase women. But during the Holocaust he saved over a thousand Jews from almost certain death by convincing Nazi officials to let him have the Jews as workers in his factories. He put the Jews' names on a list that became famous as "Schindler's list."

Oskar Schindler was born in Zwittau, Austria-Hungary (now Svitavy, Czech Republic) in 1908. The town was in a region called Sudetenland, which in 1918 became part of the new nation of Czechoslovakia. His family, like many others in

Oskar Schindler (second from the right)

Sudetenland, was Germanic in origin, and he grew up thinking of himself as a German.

After studying engineering and performing military service, he went to work for his father, who owned a farm machinery plant. In the 1930s the factory went bankrupt, and Schindler took a job as traveling sales manager of an electrical company in Brno, in the province of Moravia, Czechoslovakia. He joined the local Nazi party so that he could sell products more easily during business trips to Nazi Germany.[1]

In 1938 Germany began to break apart Schindler's homeland. In March of that year, Hitler annexed (added) Austria to Germany by sending in German troops, who met no resistance. The world feared that he would next invade Czechoslovakia. At a conference in Munich, Germany, in late September 1938, the nations of Great Britain, France, and Italy agreed to let Hitler have Sudetenland. Sudetenland lay between Germany and the rest of Czechoslovakia. On October 1 German troops occupied the region. The world hoped that Hitler would be satisfied with this prize and would let the rest of Czechoslovakia alone. But in March 1939 German troops took over Czechoslovakia's western provinces of Bohemia and Moravia. Germany allowed the remaining province, Slovakia, to become an independent state. But Slovakia was forced to provide Germany with troops, railroad service, and other wartime help.

When Hitler took over Sudetenland, Schindler, as an ethnic German, faced the possibility of being forced into the German army. To avoid that military duty, he agreed to spy for Germany while traveling in Poland in 1938 and 1939.

In 1939 the Germans invaded Poland. They took Polish businesses away from Jews and arranged for non-Jews to run the firms. Late that year Schindler moved to Krakow, Poland, where he was given control over two previously Jewish-owned companies that made and sold enamel kitchenware. Later he established his own enamel works in Zablocie, outside Krakow. By 1941 he was making huge sums of money by supplying pots and pans to the German army and by selling products on the black market.

Schindler used the profits to buy expensive liquor, clothing, jewelry, furniture, and other items. With some of these things he bribed German officials to keep him out of the army. He kept other luxuries for his own pleasure. Having left his wife, Emilie, at home in Moravia, he lived the high life in Poland. He attended many parties where he became friendly with Nazi officials, including Amon Goeth, the brutal commander of the Plaszow Jewish forced-labor camp near Krakow.

However, Schindler soon grew disgusted with the Nazis' treatment of the Jews. The SS broke into Jewish homes and robbed, beat, and killed Jews at will. One day an SS squad invaded Poland's oldest synagogue, built in the fourteenth century. They forced the Jews to spit on the Torah, a Jewish holy book. When one refused, the Nazis killed him. Then they shot to death all the other Jews and burned the synagogue. Schindler clearly saw the Nazis' real goal: to exterminate all the Jews. Furious, he resolved to rescue as many Jews as he could.[2]

Encouraged by his Jewish accountant, Isaac Stern, Schindler acquired more and more Jews to work in his factory. There he could treat them well and protect them from being sent to death camps. At first he hired individual Jews he met through Stern. Later, with liquor and luxuries, Schindler bribed Julian Scherner, the SS chief in the Krakow ghetto, to supply large numbers of Jewish workers. To help ensure their safety, Schindler made a deal with the Germans to produce antitank shells at the plant. These products were essential to the war effort, so the Nazis could not afford to kill the workers. Schindler established a night shift so that he could increase his labor force.

Many of Schindler's Jewish workers had no experience in their factory jobs. However, to save their jobs and therefore their lives, Schindler assured the Nazis that the workers were skilled. When Nazi inspectors came to examine his factory, he got them drunk so that they could not see his people fumbling at their jobs. "If you work here," he promised the Jews, "you'll live through the war."[3]

When he had to, he saved his workers from being shot or deported. Once, for example, his office

Schindler (center) enjoys himself at a dinner party with SS officials in Krakow.

manager, Abraham Bankier, and twelve of his workers were sent with other Jews to the train depot to board cattle cars destined for a death camp. Schindler rushed to the depot and argued with the SS guards, saying that these Jews performed important war-related labor for the German army. The guards reluctantly returned the men to Schindler.

Several times the Gestapo arrested him for corruption. But each time his powerful Nazi friends, including some in the German central government in Berlin, got him released.

In March 1943 the Nazis removed all the Jews from the Krakow ghetto. Those Jews able to work were transferred to the nearby Plaszow labor camp. Others were shot or shipped to Auschwitz for extermination. Schindler's Jews moved from the ghetto to Plaszow. From there they walked every day to the factory at Zablocie and back again.

One of Schindler's drinking friends was the German general in charge of producing war equipment in Poland. Schindler convinced this general to convert Plaszow's workshops from uniform mending to war-related wood and metal work. Conversion took Plaszow, at least temporarily, off the list of labor camps whose inmates were scheduled for death.

The conversion also gave higher status to the camp commander, Amon Goeth, who in gratitude granted Schindler a favor. Goeth allowed him to build a little camp near the factory. In this camp

Schindler's Jewish workers could live and be safe from the brutality at Plaszow.[4]

When the Soviet Army approached in October 1944, the Nazis planned to close Plaszow and Schindler's branch and send the inmates to a death camp. Schindler, through bribery, persuaded the Nazis to let him open an armaments production company in Sudetenland, taking with him Jews from his Zablocie factory as well as other workers from Plaszow. He made a list of about eleven hundred Jews whom he wanted for his new plant.

At first most of the eight hundred men on his list were sent by train to the Gross-Rosen concentration camp in Silesia, a region between Czechoslovakia and Poland. Soon, however, they were shipped to the new factory in Brünnlitz (now Brnener, Czech Republic). The three hundred women on the list were diverted to Auschwitz, but by November they, too, had arrived in Brünnlitz. "You have nothing more to worry about," he told them. "You're with me now."[5] The town had a labor camp, but Schindler's Jews were allowed to live at the factory in prisoners' dormitories.

During that autumn Schindler was again arrested on charges of corruption. He was taken back to Krakow in handcuffs. While he was gone, Emilie, who had joined him in Brünnlitz, carried out his plans to protect the Jews. After more than a week Schindler was released, his bribed friends once more coming to his aid.

Schindler raised the population of his group to twelve hundred when he rescued about one hundred nearly frozen Jewish prisoners from a train stranded in nearby Zwittau. The human cargo had no official destination, so Schindler boldly wrote "Zwittau" on the bill of lading. Then he took the Jews to his factory-dormitory, where they were nursed back to health, especially by Emilie. At first they were too weak to work, but, to save their lives, he paid the Nazis the same daily tax for each new arrival that he paid for every one of his working laborers.

Schindler spent his whole fortune on protecting the Jews. He bought liquor and other items to bribe the Nazis. And he supplied his workers with food, medical care, and even Nazi uniforms and weapons so that the Jews could defend themselves if necessary.

Schindler considered the Jews' emotional needs as well. For example, the Nazis wanted dead Jews burned, but Schindler secretly allowed traditional Jewish burials. He also let the Jews celebrate religious holidays.

On May 7, 1945, a radio broadcast announced that Germany was going to surrender. The war would end at midnight that night. At Schindler's request the Jews let the German guards go away peacefully.[6] On May 8, however, he armed some of the Jews and allowed them to shoot to death the local SS commander, who had threatened to kill the Jews at the last minute.[7] Soon the Nazis were gone and the Jews were safe.

Now Oskar and Emilie Schindler feared being arrested or killed by the Soviet army, which was approaching from the east. An ethnic German and officially a Nazi, he was an enemy to the Soviets. The Schindlers prepared to flee westward toward the American Army. The Americans, Schindler believed, would treat him more humanely than the Soviets would.

Schindler gave the Jews presents, including cloth to make new clothes. The Jews gave him protective letters (in German and Hebrew) saying that he had saved their lives. One of the Jews, a jeweler, made him a ring from gold dental work donated by another former prisoner. On the ring was inscribed a verse from a Jewish holy book, the Talmud: "Whoever saves a single soul, it is as if he had saved the whole world."[8] On May 9 the Schindlers left Brünnlitz with several Jews as bodyguards.

After the war Schindler struggled with poverty. He had spent his money during the war, and his property was taken by the Soviets. His new business ventures all failed. The American Joint Distribution Committee and the *Schindlerjuden* ("Schindler's Jews"), as the survivors called themselves, took care of him.

Schindler was honored as one of the Righteous Ones Among the Nations of the World on his birthday, April 28, 1962. He spent his last years in Frankfurt, Germany, and died there in October 1974. At his own request, he was buried in a

Catholic cemetery in Jerusalem. Over four hundred Jews—*Schindlerjuden* and their families—attended the service.

"I knew the people who worked for me," he said in the 1960s. "When you know people, you have to behave towards them like human beings."[9]

Andrew Sheptitsky

7

Andrew Sheptitsky
Greek Catholic Rescuer

As head of the Greek Catholic (Uniate) Church in southeast Poland, Andrew Sheptitsky spoke out against the brutal treatment of Jews. His views influenced many ordinary citizens to protect Jews from Nazis and other anti-Semites. He arranged for over one hundred and fifty Jews to take refuge in convents, monasteries, his church, and even his own home.

Andrew Sheptitsky was born into an aristocratic Polish family in 1865. In 1888 he joined the Basilian order of the Greek Catholic faith. In 1899 he was appointed a bishop, and the following year he became the metropolitan (leader) of the Uniate church in southeast Poland, centered in Lwow.

In Lwow, Andrew Sheptitsky devoted himself to church matters during his first eighteen years as metropolitan. However, in 1918, at the end of World War I, he began to take a leading role in political affairs. Eastern Poland, bordering Ukraine, had a large population of Ukrainians, many of whom belonged to Sheptitsky's church. He became a spokesman in their struggle for Ukrainian national rights.[1]

The Ukrainian people developed a national identity as early as the thirteenth century, but their land was constantly under foreign rule. From 1795 to 1918 most of Ukraine was under Russian control. After World War I, Russia underwent the Communist revolution and became the Soviet Union. Ukraine took advantage of the situation to establish the independent, non-Communist Ukrainian People's Republic. But the Soviet Army soon crushed the Ukrainians' new government.

In 1920 the Soviets went to war with Poland in yet another struggle for territory. This war proved to be a disaster for the Ukrainians. When the war ended, Poland's border extended into western Ukrainian lands. Meanwhile, the Soviets took control of the eastern and central regions of Ukraine and forced them into the Soviet Union as the Ukrainian Republic.

Ukrainians in both Poland and the Soviet Union suffered. In Polish-held areas that were historically Ukrainian, such as Lwow, great tensions developed between Ukrainians and their rulers. Ukrainians organized their own military units and prepared to fight for freedom. In the Soviet Union, conditions were even worse. The Soviets, under the dictator Josef Stalin, tried to stamp out Ukrainian traditions and to replace them with the Soviet Communist system. When Ukrainians resisted, the Soviets took Ukrainian property and deported tens of thousands of families to the frozen wasteland of Siberia. During 1932–1933 the Soviets confiscated food in Ukraine, starving to death over 5 million people.

In 1939, Germany and the Soviet Union attacked Poland and divided the conquered country. The Soviets took over the western Ukraine and incorporated it into the Ukrainian Republic. Most of the Ukrainians were now united, but they were under the tyranny of the hated Soviets.

Throughout their troubled history, the Ukrainians maintained a deep hatred for Jews. From at least the sixteenth century, there was a large Jewish population in the region. One reason for the anti-Semitism was that the Ukrainians were largely Christian and had the same prejudices that other Christians had against Jews. In addition, Ukrainian nobility used Jews to collect taxes from the people. Poor peasants were especially hurt by these taxes and developed a great hatred for the Jewish tax collectors. Violence often erupted against Jews during the succeeding centuries. In 1919–1920, for example, about sixty thousand Jews were killed in Ukraine. By 1939

Sheptitsky was very old when he began to help the Jews.

hatred of Jews in the region was reaching a boiling point. In the Ukrainians' struggle for independence from Poland, both the Poles and the Ukrainians accused Jews of helping the other side.

By 1939 Andrew Sheptitsky was an elderly man with a long white beard. He was partially paralyzed and confined to a wheelchair. But he still had great influence in eastern Poland, especially in the Ukrainian community.

When the German army entered Lwow in June 1941, Sheptitsky praised the Germans for liberating the Ukrainians from the Soviets. He hoped that, supported by Nazi Germany, an independent Ukraine would be formed. Sheptitsky urged the Ukrainians to cooperate with the Germans. He himself supported the formation of a Ukrainian army division that worked with the Nazi forces, and he appointed one of his closest aides to serve as chief chaplain of the division.

But with Nazi occupation, local Ukrainian thugs felt free to let their own hatred of Jews have full rein. Ukrainians began imprisoning, torturing, and killing Jews. Even though he was a spokesman for the anti-Semitic Ukrainians, Sheptitsky had long had close relations with Jewish leaders in his region. In July 1941, Rabbi Ezekiel Lewin went to Sheptitsky, who promised to try to restrain the Ukrainian violence. Rabbi Lewin himself was attacked and killed by Ukrainians on his way home from the meeting.[2]

Sheptitsky issued messages to the Ukrainian people, warning them against committing murder.[3]

His pleas culminated in a November 1942 pastoral letter titled "Thou Shalt Not Murder," aimed at those who killed either Jews or rival Ukrainians.[4] He threatened "divine punishment" for offenders who would "shed innocent blood and make of themselves outcasts of human society by disregarding the sanctity of man."[5] The metropolitan banned religious services for those who accepted murder.

He also spoke out to the Germans. When an official of the German foreign ministry visited him, Sheptitsky condemned the Nazis' treatment of the Jews. In February 1942 he wrote a letter to Heinrich Himmler, head of the SS, asking him to stop the Ukrainian police's participation in the murder of Jews.

But he did not stop with verbal efforts. On August 14, 1942, Sheptitsky set into motion a new plan: hiding Jews. He was visited that day by two rabbis who asked him if he would store their Torah scrolls at his church and find a hiding place for some Jewish children. He agreed and also sought the help of his brother, Father Superior Clement Sheptitsky, who headed the Uniate monasteries, and of his sister, Sister Josepha, who led the Uniate nunneries. Together, they hid over one hundred and fifty Jewish children and adults in convents, monasteries, and churches. Hundreds of nuns and monks knew about the hidden Jews, but no one ever betrayed the secret. Sheptitsky hid fifteen Jews in his own residence, even though it was often visited by German officials.[6]

"I want you to be a good Jew," he once explained to a Jewish man who hid in a monastery, sometimes disguised as a monk, "and I am not saving you for your own sake. I am saving you for your people. I do not expect any reward, nor do I expect you to accept my faith."[7]

By word and deed, Sheptitsky influenced many Ukrainians in Poland to help Jews. Even while some Ukrainians were killing Jews, others, following the example of their metropolitan, were saving the persecuted ones by offering shelter and other aid.

While carrying out his humanitarian acts toward the Jews, Sheptitsky also maintained his long-standing position as a spokesman for the Ukrainian population. These two roles—one in favor of the Jews and one in favor of the Ukrainians—forced him to take some contradictory positions. For the sake of the Ukrainians, he praised and cooperated with the Nazis. But for the sake of the Jews, he confronted and deceived the Nazis. Sheptitsky's compassion for the Jews and his support for the Ukrainian nationalists formed a pair of opposing responsibilities that he could never resolve.[8] Shortly after the Soviets drove the Germans out of Poland in August 1944, he died.

The Jews whom he saved saw no contradiction in Andrew Sheptitsky. "In 1942, when I found that the situation was hopeless," remembered one of the rescued, "I visited Metropolitan [Sheptitsky] and asked him for help. . . . Almost immediately he began a planned campaign to save lives."[9]

Sempo Sugihara

8

Sempo Sugihara
Japanese Diplomat Rescuer

Disobeying his own government's direct orders, the Japanese diplomat Sempo Sugihara issued visas to thousands of Jews in Kaunas, the capital of Lithuania. The visas allowed the Jews, who feared both German and Soviet invaders, to travel through Japan to the safety of other countries. Because Japan was a World War II ally of Nazi Germany, Sugihara should have regarded Jews as enemies. His pro-Jewish action put his career and even his life at risk. Even though his government eventually fired him and prevented him from getting another good job, he never regretted helping the Jews.

Sempo Sugihara was born in Yaotsu, Japan, on January 1, 1900. Both of his parents originally had the surname of Iwai. His mother was Yatsu Iwai, from a noble line of Iwais who dated back to the feudal lord of the region. Sugihara's father was Mitsugoro Iwai. It was Mitsugoro's decision to change his first name to Kosui and the family name to Sugihara. As Kosui Sugihara, he worked for the Japanese government. First he was a local tax collector. Later he went to Korea, where he helped to administer colonies established there by Japan. After he left government service, he stayed in Korea and opened his own Japanese-style inn.

Sempo Sugihara grew up and performed his World War II deeds under the name of Chiune Sugihara. By the 1960s, he had changed it to Sempo Sugiwara, another possible reading of the Japanese characters representing his name.[1] However, he came to be universally known as Sempo Sugihara.

He studied from 1919 to 1920 at the Harbin Gakuin in northern China. The Harbin Gakuin was an academy where Japan trained experts on the Soviet Union. After serving from 1920 to 1922 in the Japanese military, Sugihara returned to the Harbin Gakuin as an instructor of the Russian language.

Sugihara married a Russian woman, Klaudia Semionovna Apollonova, and adopted the Russian Orthodox religion. After divorcing Klaudia he married a Japanese woman, Yukiko Kikuchi, in 1936.

Like his father, Sempo Sugihara decided to enter Japanese government service. After joining the Japanese diplomatic corps, he spent several years engaged in secret foreign affairs assignments. The Japanese government needed his services, especially his knowledge of the Russian language, in Lithuania. In August 1939 Germany and the Soviet Union signed an agreement not to attack each other. The two nations also carved up eastern Europe, each taking control of certain areas. Lithuania, while remaining independent, fell under the influence of the Soviets. Because of this influence, the Soviets were allowed to establish military bases in Lithuania.

At about this time, Japan was planning to make its own military agreement with Germany. However, before Japan would make such an agreement, it wanted to know more about the German-Soviet pact.

In early September 1939 the Japanese government sent Sempo Sugihara to Kaunas. As a consul he was supposed to represent Japanese business interests. But in fact he was there to spy on German and Soviet activities. For the next nine months, he was busily engaged in that service.

In June 1940 the Soviet army took control of Lithuania. In July the invaders formally incorporated the occupied country into the Soviet Union. Sugihara reported to Tokyo that the Soviets were treating people harshly, especially Jews.[2] The Jews also feared an invasion by the Germans, who would kill them outright.

Two Dutch Jews studying in Kaunas finally found a possible way of escape. They asked the local

Sugihara and his family in the Japanese Consulate in Kaunas (Kovno), Lithuania, shortly after their arrival. Seated from left to right are sister-in-law Setsuko Kikuchi, Sempo Sugihara, son Chiaki, son Hiroki, and Sempo's wife, Yukiko Sugihara.

Dutch consul, Jan Zwartendijk, for help. He gave
them permits to enter the Dutch island of Curaçao
in the Caribbean and agreed to give similar permission to Polish Jews stranded in Kaunas. (The Polish
Jews had fled to Lithuania when Germany invaded
Poland in 1939.) Having an official destination
available to them allowed the Jews to ask other consuls for transit visas so that the Jews could travel
through the consuls' countries on the way to
Curaçao.

Because the Germans were coming from the
west, the Jews planned to travel east through the
Soviet Union and then through Japan to the free
world. However, Soviet authorities said that they
would agree to the plan only if the refugees could
obtain transit visas from Japan.[3] The key person in
the escape, then, was the Japanese consul.

In July 1940 a group of Jewish refugees headed
by Dr. Zorah Warhaftig (years later a minister in the
Israeli government) explained the situation to
Sugihara, who was willing to help. First, however, he
had to seek his government's approval.

Japan's attitude toward Jews differed from that of
Germany. Even though the Japanese believed much
of the Nazi anti-Jewish propaganda, they did not
have the Germans' deep hatred for Jews.

In fact, during World War II, Japan legally protected Jewish refugees who fled Nazi Germany or the
Soviet Union and managed to reach Japanese-held
areas of China. The Japanese truly believed the

anti-Semitic idea that Jews had great international financial power. One of the great heroes in Japan was the American Jewish banker Jacob Schiff, who arranged loans that helped Japan to win its war with Russia in 1905. The Japanese, then, had a practical attitude toward Jews: believe the worst about them, but treat them with care because their money and international connections might be useful someday.

Before his experiences in Kaunas, Sempo Sugihara showed no particular feeling for or against Jews. When the Jewish refugees asked him for visas, he cabled Tokyo several times for permission to grant the documents. But his superiors repeatedly rejected the plan. At that time, Japan was close to entering a military alliance with Germany. German officials were putting pressure on the Japanese to cooperate with them in disposing of Jews, not helping the refugees to escape.

Sugihara regarded himself as a loyal servant of his homeland. But if he obeyed his government's orders, the Jews would surely be murdered by the approaching Germans. For two nights he worried and could not sleep. "I cannot allow these people to die," he finally thought to himself, "people who have come to me for help with death staring them in the eyes. Whatever punishment may be imposed on me [for disobeying government instructions], I know I should follow my conscience."[4]

Sugihara began issuing transit visas without his government's approval. On July 30 alone, he granted

257 of them. For a couple of weeks he continued to try to get Tokyo's official permission, but on August 3, the Soviets ordered him to close his consulate within the month. Time was running out. "On the 10th of August," he later recalled, "I finally decided that it was completely useless to continue the discussions with Tokyo." Beginning on August 11, "I gave visa[s] to all who came to me, regardless of the fact whether or not they could produce some kind of document proving they were going to another country via Japan."[5]

Long lines of Jews formed in the street in front of the Japanese consulate. Sugihara worked tirelessly, keeping the office open longer hours and writing transit visas as fast as he could. At night his hands were so stiff that his wife, Yukiko, had to massage them back to life. She shared her husband's stress, becoming unable to nurse their newborn son. To speed up the production of the visas, Sugihara's assistants made rubber stamps for filling in parts of the documents. Jews themselves were sometimes invited into the office to help process the papers.[6]

When the Japanese government discovered that Sugihara was issuing the transit visas, it ordered him to stop. But he ignored his superiors.

Among those he rescued, besides Warhaftig, was Menahem Savidor, who later became a leader in the Knesset (Israel's parliament). Sugihara also saved the entire staff and student body of the famous Mir yeshiva (a Jewish religious school). Founded over one hundred and twenty years earlier in the Polish city of Mir, the yeshiva community had fled to Lithuania in 1939 when Hitler's troops invaded Poland. Because of Sugihara's efforts, Mir was the only one of Europe's twenty major yeshivas to survive the war.[7]

Sugihara knew that the Polish Jews had no intention of going to Curaçao, but he cooperated with them anyway to save their lives. From Kaunas the Jews crossed the Soviet Union by train, went by boat to Japan, and after spending some time in China and other countries eventually reached Palestine (later Israel) and the United States.

Late in August the Soviet authorities, intending to remove all foreign consular representatives from Kaunas, forced Sugihara to close his office. However, he continued his rescue operation from a hotel room where he stayed for a few days. As he, Yukiko, and their three children were on their way to the railroad station to leave Kaunas in early September, he still wrote out visas. Even as the train was pulling away from the station, he was signing papers and thrusting them out the window.

Sugihara made a list of the people he rescued. The existing Kaunas list is incomplete, but it shows that he issued at least 2,139 visas. An entire family could travel on one visa, so he may have saved the lives of as many as ten thousand Jews.[8]

The Jews to whom Sugihara gave transit visas escaped. But those who remained in Lithuania were not so lucky. In June 1941, the Germans, breaking their agreement not to attack the Soviet Union, drove the Soviets out of Kaunas. The Nazis and their Lithuanian collaborators slaughtered thousands of Jews over the next few years before the Soviet Army recaptured the city in August 1944.

Meanwhile, Sugihara and his family went from Kaunas to Berlin, Germany. He arrived there in early September 1940 and was soon sent to the consulate in Prague, Czechoslovakia. In February 1941, he was transferred to Königsberg, in the German state of Prussia. In December of that year he was assigned to Bucharest, Romania, where he stayed until the end of the war. At these other cities, he continued to issue visas to Jews who wanted to escape. Again he kept lists of the people to whom he granted visas.[9] These Nazi-occupied cities were even more dangerous for him than Soviet-occupied Kaunas had been. Nazis did not hesitate to kill anyone helping Jews.

In August 1944 the Soviets captured Romania. For a year and a half after the war, they held Sugihara because he had spied on Russians in Bucharest.

Returning to Japan in 1947, Sugihara was forced out of diplomatic service and was denied an official recommendation for work in private business. Government authorities told him that he was being treated this way because he had disobeyed orders by helping the Jews in Kaunas. His whole family suffered social rejection by other Japanese. For many years he moved from one minor job to another. Finally, in

1961 a Japanese exporting company hired him and sent him as their sales representative to Moscow.

After retiring, he lived on Tokyo Bay. He died in Kamakura, near Tokyo, on July 31, 1986.

In his last years he was often asked about his activities in Kaunas. "Someone had to make a sacrifice to save all those lives," he once explained. "I looked at all those people clinging to the iron fences of the consulate begging for visas, and I thought I just had to do something for them. In pure joy, they would fall to their knees in thanks. I was so inspired by the sight that I worked non-stop for a month writing visas."[10]

Marion van Binsbergen Pritchard

Dutch Rescuer of Children

As a young student of social work in Amsterdam, Holland, Marion van Binsbergen (later Pritchard) saw Nazi atrocities that made her weep and shake with rage. Repeatedly risking her life to save others, she even murdered a Nazi to protect Jews. She later wished that she had been able to rescue more, but she probably saved about one hundred and fifty people, many of them small children.

Marion van Binsbergen was born in 1920. From her father, a judge in Amsterdam, she learned to have tolerance toward differences in other people. From her mother, who was tough and confident, she learned to be action-oriented. Both of these qualities—sensitivity and aggressiveness—blossomed in her when she became a rescuer during the Holocaust.

Marion van Binsbergen Pritchard

As a child she attended a private school where Jewish and gentile students mixed freely. "In Holland," she later said, "the Jews were considered Dutch like everyone else."[1]

The Dutch were a peaceful people and had a tradition of neutrality during military conflicts. In World War I, for example, Holland remained neutral. But after the German army invaded Holland in 1940, the country was forced to serve the German side in World War II.

The invasion began on the night of May 19–20, 1940. Four days later the Dutch army surrendered. Queen Wilhelmina and her government escaped to London, England. Arthur Seyss-Inquart, an Austrian statesman, administered the new German-dominated government. He canceled the Dutch parliament and appointed Dutch Nazis to help him run the country. The Germans intended eventually to incorporate Holland into their Reich as a Germanic state.

But Dutch citizens resisted even after their army surrendered. Their open resistance climaxed on February 25, 1941, with a general strike. The Dutch refused to go to their jobs because they felt that their work supported the Germans. The German army ended the strike by brutally forcing people back to work. After the strike, Dutch resistance went underground. Individuals and small groups secretly did what they could to disrupt the Germans' plans in Holland. The Germans continued to respond to that resistance with acts of terror. They stole goods from factories and they seized food. They sent thousands of Dutch citizens to Germany as forced labor, and they executed Dutch hostages. They bombed Dutch cities, including Amsterdam. Holland was finally liberated by the Allies in May 1945.

Before the German invasion, there were 140,000 Jews in Holland. About 110,000 were Dutch while 30,000 were refugees from Germany and Austria. Nearly 60 percent of the Jews lived in Amsterdam. Dutch Jews enjoyed full equality in the political and cultural life of the country.

Soon after the Germans took control of Holland, however, the German and Dutch Nazis began to persecute the Jews. In February 1941 a violent incident occurred between a group of Jews and a German police patrol. A few days later the Germans arrested four hundred Jews and deported them to a Nazi concentration camp in Mauthausen, Austria. This treatment of the Jews was one of the reasons for the Dutch general strike of February 25. And one of the ways in which the Nazis stopped the strike was to threaten to arrest and deport more Jews. Soon the Nazis began to take away Jewish property and to restrict Jews' activities. In January 1942 forced-labor camps for Jews were set up. In July the Nazis began to deport Jews to Auschwitz and other death camps. Again the Dutch protested. But again the Nazis stopped the protests by making arrests and threatening even more violence. By the end of the Holocaust, the Nazis had killed at least 75 percent of all the Jews in Holland.

When the Nazis invaded Holland in 1940, van Binsbergen was a student at the school of social work in Amsterdam. She and her family were among the resisters. One way to resist was by not cooperating. For example, the Nazis wanted the Dutch to fill out papers identifying themselves as Jews or non-Jews. "If you were Jewish you filled out one form," she later explained, "and if you were Aryan, as they call it, you filled out another. My father refused to sign the form, as did I."[2]

One day in 1941 she was visiting and studying at a friend's apartment. Unknown to her, the students who lived there made and distributed copies of Allied radio broadcasts. For this offense the Nazis stormed in and arrested the students and van Binsbergen. She spent seven months in prison. "I always thought I had my mother's ability to ignore fear," she later said, "until I spent some time in jail and that was very frightening."[3]

In 1942, after her release, van Binsbergen was doing social work in a rehabilitation center. One day, the woman in charge, fearing that a Jewish family would soon be taken, asked her to take the family's two-year-old boy home. Van Binsbergen kept the boy at her parents' home for several months. She never told them that he was Jewish, and they never asked. Eventually, she found the child a safer place to hide outside Amsterdam.

Ambitious to become a psychoanalyst, van Binsbergen was preparing for this career by having herself analyzed. By this time she was already involved with trying to help people avoid being sent to concentration camps. Now her analyst, who was Jewish, asked her for help, and she provided it by finding a hiding place for him and by taking him food, clothing, and news. Ultimately, however, he was discovered and did not survive.

One day van Binsbergen was riding her bicycle to school when she stopped at a small Jewish children's home. She saw Nazis loading children into trucks for deportation to camps. "When they didn't move fast enough," she later remembered, "a Nazi would pick them up by an arm or a leg or even hair and throw them onto the trucks."[4] Two women came along and tried to prevent this outrage, but they, too, were thrown into a truck. "When I saw that, I knew that my rescue work was more important than anything else I might be doing."[5] And, because of the fate of the two women who tried to help the children, she realized that a direct confrontation with the Nazis was useless. She must work completely in secret.

Van Binsbergen devoted herself to the welfare of Jews by providing them with hiding places, false identity papers, food, clothing, ration cards, and medical care.[6] She often had to place children in locations separate from those of their parents. "People would take one person but not two," she later explained, "a child but not an adult, or an adult but no children."[7]

In one case, a pregnant woman was hiding with her husband. The people keeping them could not have a baby in the apartment. So van Binsbergen asked another couple if they would temporarily take the baby when it was born. They agreed, and the woman pretended to be pregnant. But the baby, a boy, was delivered prematurely. The nurse who took care of the couple's four other children was not immediately available. So van Binsbergen stayed for a week and cared for the newborn until the nurse arrived.

In another case, she made a long train ride with a baby girl in her arms to a small town in northern Holland. She was to give the infant to a certain person for safekeeping. At the train station, a man told her that that person had been arrested. He invited her to his home to rest. She soon fell asleep, and when she awoke she found the man's wife changing and feeding the baby. The couple immediately decided to keep the baby themselves. To explain the baby to their other children and to neighbors, the couple said, according to van Binsbergen, that "I was a sinner, that I had this baby out of wedlock, and that my punishment was that they were going to keep the baby, and I would never see it again."[8]

In 1942 she was asked by her friends in the resistance to find a hiding place for a man, Freddie Pollak, and his three small children, two boys and a girl. Van Binsbergen moved them into a large house in the country. The house belonged to an elderly lady

Marion van Binsbergen Pritchard hid Freddie Pollack and his three children from 1942 till the end of the war. Here she is shown holding Pollack's daughter, Erica.

whose son-in-law was a friend of Freddie's. For one year she visited them only on weekends. But in 1943 she decided to live with them full-time so that she could provide more help in caring for the children. She told the neighbors that the children were hers.

Pollak and van Binsbergen removed some floorboards under a rug and built a hiding place in the basement. The father and children hid there during Nazi raids. One night four Germans and one Dutch Nazi policeman searched the house while the Jews hid under the floor. After the Nazis left, the family began climbing out of the hiding place. Just then, the Dutch Nazi unexpectedly returned. "When the Dutch policeman came back, I had to kill him with a revolver a friend had given me but I had never expected to use," van Binsbergen later recalled. "I know I had no choice, but I still wish there had been some other way."[9] A local undertaker helped her dispose of the corpse by putting it into a coffin with another body.

During this period she often wished that she could do more for others. "There were times that the fear got the better of me," she later admitted, "and I did not do something I could have."[10] Despite that feeling, however, she did continue to help other Jews in distress.

In July 1944, for example, she helped to rescue a little girl from a doctor's home where Nazis had temporarily confined her. While a Jewish accomplice occupied the doctor and the Nazi guard in one part of the house, van Binsbergen slipped into another part of the home and found the girl. "I grabbed her, ran down the stairs, put her on the back of my bike, and pedaled off. It seemed as though she knew how high the stakes were. She was so small, so brave, and so scared, but she didn't utter a sound."[11] The girl survived the war.

Van Binsbergen returned to the Pollaks. They, too, made it to the liberation.

After the war she took a job with the United Nations Relief and Rehabilitation Administration and worked in displaced-persons camps, hoping to find information about her Jewish friends. One camp was run by Tony Pritchard, an American. They married in 1947. In that same year she moved with him to the United States. They had three sons.

In America her dream of becoming a psychoanalyst finally came true. She made a special study of altruistic behavior, which means helping people without expecting anything in return. Marion van Binsbergen Pritchard believes that such behavior originates in families where parents are good role models who make sacrifices for the welfare of their children[12] and who treat the young ones with respect and consideration.[13]

For many years she did not talk about her experiences during World War II. In recent years, however, she has come to believe in remembering and telling. "But it's difficult," she admits; "I still find myself weepy when I retell a story."[14]

10

Raoul Wallenberg

"I Want to Save a Nation"

Raoul Wallenberg was a Swedish diplomat who issued passports that protected thousands of Jews in Budapest, Hungary. But Wallenberg, dedicated to saving as many Hungarian Jews as possible, went far beyond simply processing paperwork. He risked his life many times in face-to-face confrontations with German and Hungarian officials. Sometimes he literally snatched Jews out of Nazi hands through his bold use of persuasion, bribery, blackmail, threats, and pure bluff (in cases where he had no real authority or influence). In the end, he personally saved the lives of tens of thousands of Hungarian Jews and became a legendary figure.

Raoul Gustaf Wallenberg was born in Kapptsta, near Stockholm, Sweden, on August 4, 1912. His

Raoul Wallenberg

family was well known in Sweden for its long line of successful businessmen, diplomats, and naval officers. The Wallenberg family owned the Enskilda Bank. Raoul Oscar Wallenberg, his father, was a naval officer who died of cancer before young Raoul was born. Maj, his mother, later married a man named Fredrik von Dardel.

As a child Raoul Wallenberg showed that he was sensitive to cruelty and was willing to act on his beliefs. He hated hunting because it led to the killing of animals. So one night before a hunt he broke into his neighbors' kennels and released the hunting dogs. He also showed courage. In one instance, during a thunderstorm when he was a small child, while others hid he ran outside and shouted, "Let's see God's fireworks!"[1]

As a youth Wallenberg traveled widely and learned the English, French, German, and Russian languages in addition to his native Swedish. From 1931 to 1935 he studied architecture in the United States at the University of Michigan. After graduating in early 1935, he returned to Sweden for a brief reunion with his family. He then served as a trainee with a Swedish trading company in South Africa and with a Dutch bank in Haifa, Palestine.

During his six months in Palestine, he met Jews who had fled Hitler's Germany. "What he learned from them of Nazi persecution moved him deeply— not only because he was a warm, sympathetic man, but also because he knew his great-great-grandfather on his mother's side had been a Jew."[2] Wallenberg's Jewish ancestor was Michael Benedicks,[3] who, in the late 1700s, was one of the first Jews to settle in Sweden. Because of Benedicks, Wallenberg's "maternal grandmother, in whose home he was raised, was one-quarter Jewish—enough of a Jew, had she lived in Hungary, to be included in Eichmann's transports [to death camps]," Frederick E. Werbell and Clarke Thurston point out. "This was one reason why he became so agitated whenever anyone mentioned the persecution of the European Jews."[4] As early as 1930 Wallenberg revealed his feelings about being one-sixteenth Jewish to his friend Ingemar Hedenius, later one of Sweden's leading academic philosophers. "He was proud of his partial Jewish ancestry," Hedenius recorded in 1980, "and, as I recall, must have exaggerated it somewhat. I remember him saying, 'A person like me, who is both a Wallenberg and half-Jewish, can never be defeated.'"[5]

Wallenberg returned to Sweden from Palestine in the fall of 1936. He wanted to go into the field of architecture, but his American architecture degree did not qualify him for such work in Sweden. So over the next several years he engaged in various business ventures. In 1941, he became the foreign sales representative of the Central European Trading Company, a firm headed by Koloman Lauer, a Hungarian Jew. Lauer, as a Jew, could not travel in Nazi-occupied Europe. So he hired Wallenberg, a pleasant man with a knowledge of several European languages, to make sales for the company throughout Europe.

By then World War II was already two years old. Lauer's homeland, Hungary, was led by Admiral Miklós Horthy. In 1938 Horthy, fearing an invasion by Nazi Germany, tried to make friends with Hitler by setting up anti-Jewish laws in Hungary. In 1939 Hungary became a World War II ally of Germany. But when Hitler began his campaign of mass murder against Jews, Horthy avoided helping the Nazis. Jews from Nazi-occupied Poland, Czechoslovakia, and elsewhere poured into Hungary for Horthy's protection. Finally, however, an impatient Hitler decided to take the Hungarian Jewish matter into his own hands.

On March 19, 1944, Hitler sent troops into Hungary to round up Jews. Within a few months the Germans and local authorities sent over 400,000 Jews to death camps, mostly to Auschwitz. The remaining Jews, over 200,000 of them, were trapped in the nation's capital, Budapest. Adolf Eichmann, the Nazi in charge of the deportations to the death camps, next planned to take the Budapest Jews. However, Admiral Horthy's Hungarian government, under international pressure, temporarily stopped the deportations.

In June 1944 the United States War Refugee Board and world Jewish groups wanted to send someone to rescue the Jews in Budapest. But America was at war with Hungary, so the rescuer had to come from a neutral country. Sweden agreed to send a special diplomat whose sole purpose would be to rescue Jews.

For this assignment, Lauer recommended Wallenberg, who spoke German and understood Nazi ways, having already made business trips to German-occupied countries, including Hungary. Germany was losing the war, and Wallenberg felt that some German and Hungarian officials were beginning to fear postwar punishment for what they did to the Jews. He believed that he could change some of the officials' actions by pressuring them with threats and bribery.[6] After being assured by the Swedes and the Americans that he could use any methods he chose, Wallenberg accepted the risky mission. At his farewell dinner he said, "I am going to leave you now for one reason: to save as many lives as possible; to rescue Jews from the claws of those murderers."[7] On July 9 he arrived in Budapest with the official title of second secretary at the Swedish Embassy.

Even before Wallenberg's arrival, Swedish diplomats in Budapest had helped Jews by issuing them two kinds of documents. The first was a provisional passport, given to a Jew with close family or business ties to Sweden. When Hungary discouraged this practice, the Swedes issued a visa certificate, which allowed travel to Sweden. The Hungarian authorities agreed to treat the holders of these documents as Swedish citizens. Therefore, Jews with Swedish provisional passports or visa certificates were not deported to death camps. After the deportations were temporarily stopped in early July, the documents were still important because Jews holding them were exempt from certain harsh conditions, such as being confined in detention centers. About seven hundred such passports and certificates had been issued by early July.[8]

Wallenberg, however, wanted to save not just hundreds but thousands. To trick the Nazis into accepting large numbers of these papers, he designed a new, impressive-looking document called a *Schutz-Pass* ("Protective Pass"), with seals, stamps, three royal Swedish crowns, and bold blue-and-yellow colors. It was not valid in international law. But in the eyes of the German and Hungarian authorities in Budapest, the document gave status to any Jew who held it.[9] At the Swedish Embassy, Wallenberg set up a special section where hundreds of Jews processed thousands of the protective passports. Soon other neutral diplomatic missions, such as the Swiss, the Spanish, and the Portuguese, began to issue similar documents. Wallenberg himself coordinated and led the efforts of all the neutral countries in the rescue operation.[10]

"There is endless suffering to try to ease in this place," he wrote in a July 29 memo.[11] He rented or bought buildings, where he housed Jews under the protection of Sweden and other neutral countries and provided the people there with food, clothing,

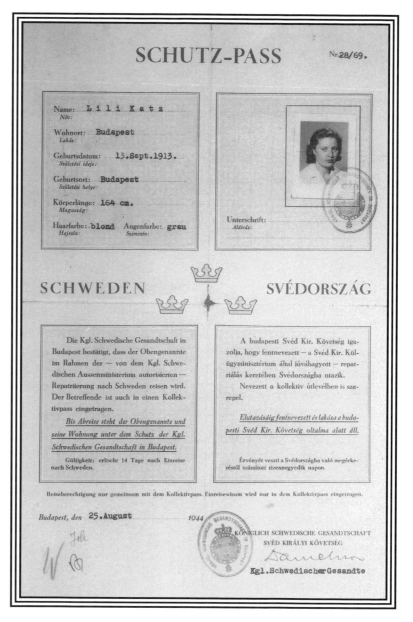

A letter of protection (*Schutz-Pass*) issued by the Swedish legation in Budapest to the Hungarian Jew Lili Katz. The document bears the initial *W* for Wallenberg in the bottom left corner.

and medicine. These buildings were known as the international ghetto to distinguish it from Budapest's central ghetto, where the Nazis kept the other Jews.

In the fall of 1944 Admiral Horthy tried to reestablish his authority in Hungary. He insisted that the Germans return the handling of Jewish affairs to his government. At first the Germans agreed. Eichmann returned to Berlin. But when they learned of Horthy's plans to make a separate peace with the Allies, the Germans forced him out of office. On October 15, the Hungarian Nazi party replaced Horthy's moderate government. Now Nazis, both German and Hungarian, began to arrest and murder Jews at will. Eichmann, returning to Budapest, planned more deportations. Wallenberg took action. He hurried the processing of thousands of protective passports, and he organized commando squads of young Jews to protect their neighbors against the Nazi thugs.[12]

The new government announced that Hungarian Jews holding protective passports would no longer be safe. Again Wallenberg acted. He went to Baroness Elizabeth Kemény, wife of the Hungarian minister of foreign affairs. Wallenberg warned her that after the war most Hungarian Nazi leaders, including her husband, would be hanged as war criminals. The only way for her husband to save his life, Wallenberg said, was to act humanely now. The baroness persuaded her husband to convince the new government to recognize the protective passports. (After the war a

Hungarian "people's court" convicted Baron Kemény of treason for his work as a Nazi. He was executed.)

Eichmann still intended to kill the Jews not holding the documents. His first step was to organize the infamous "death marches." The railroad west from Budapest to Austria and Germany was bombed out, so Eichmann forced an estimated 76,000 Jews—freezing, starving, and beaten—to march west over one hundred miles to the Austrian border. His stated purpose was to provide slave labor for the Germans. But he deliberately planned the operation so that the Jews would die either during the march or within a few months of hard labor. Escorted by Hungarian guards, large numbers of marching Jews died from cold, disease, or starvation. Some were shot to death. Others committed suicide. When the survivors reached the border, Germans took over, sending the Jews to concentration camps. The marches began on November 8, 1944, and lasted for a month.

Wallenberg and his coworkers distributed food, clothing, and medicine to the marchers till the Nazis forbade him to do so. He found some Jews with protective passports and issued new passports to other Jews on the spot. Wallenberg convinced the Nazis to let him take these Jews back to Budapest. In this way he saved thousands of Jews from Nazi labor service and death camps, even removing some after they had already boarded trains. His fearless, self-assured manner bluffed the Nazis, even Eichmann. But it broke his heart to leave so many behind. "I am sorry," he whispered to some he left on the road. "I am trying to take the youngest ones first. I want to save a nation."[13]

The undocumented Jews remaining in Budapest were required to dig trenches for the German army. Those too weak to work stayed in the ghetto.

Hungarian Nazis invaded Swedish protected houses and began dragging out the Jews. Wallenberg rushed to the scene. "This is Swedish protected territory!" he shouted. "If you want to take them you will have to shoot me first!"[14] The Jews were released.

In December the Soviet army neared Budapest. Panicky German and Hungarian Nazis attacked the remaining Jews. Again Wallenberg saved many Jews by personally confronting the Nazi bands. Some Nazis threatened to kill him; even Eichmann had made such threats. Still he went on with his work. "My life is one life," he said, "but this is a matter of saving thousands of lives."[15]

In early January 1945 the Nazis were still trying to ship Jews by train to camps. Wallenberg sometimes arranged for Aryan-looking Jews to dress up in Nazi uniforms, raid detention centers, and free large numbers of Jews while pretending to take them away for deportation.[16]

Just before the Soviets entered Budapest, the German and Hungarian Nazis made last-minute plans to blow up all the Jews in both ghettos. Wallenberg, by threats of postwar punishment and other means, prevented the operations.

In mid-January the Soviets captured the city. Wallenberg wanted to speak with Soviet authorities to ensure proper care for the liberated Jews. On January 17 he left Budapest by car with a driver and two Soviet officers. He then disappeared. Soviet officials later admitted that he had been arrested as a German spy and claimed that he had died of a heart attack in a Soviet prison in July 1947. However, former Soviet prisoners said they had seen him alive as late as the 1970s. After the Soviet Union collapsed in 1991, Soviet archives were opened. But researchers have not found any document that definitely answers the questions of when, where, and how he died.[17]

Wallenberg had personally rescued at least 20,000 Jews.[18] And by stopping the last-minute bombing of the Budapest ghettos, he had saved the entire remaining Jewish ghetto population of nearly 100,000 (about 70,000 in the central ghetto and 25,000 in the international ghetto).[19] Another 25,000 survived by hiding outside the ghettos. Largely because of Raoul Wallenberg, Budapest had the only Jewish community of substantial size left in all of Europe.

Chapter Notes

Introduction

1. Barbara Rogasky, *Smoke and Ashes: The Story of the Holocaust* (New York: Holiday House, 1988), pp. 11–12.

2. Milton Meltzer, *Rescue: The Story of How Gentiles Saved Jews in the Holocaust* (New York: Harper & Row, 1988), p. 5.

Chapter 1. Anna Borkowska: "Mother" of the Jews

1. Eric Silver, *The Book of the Just: The Unsung Heroes Who Rescued Jews from Hitler* (New York: Grove Press, 1992), p. 99.

2. Ibid., p. 102.

3. Mordecai Paldiel, *Sheltering the Jews: Stories of Holocaust Rescuers* (Minneapolis: Fortress Press, 1996), p. 35.

4. Lucy S. Dawidowicz, *The War Against the Jews, 1933–1945*, 10th anniversary ed. (New York: Seth Press, 1986), p. 314.

5. Silver, p. 100.

6. Ibid., p. 101.

7. Ibid., p. 100.

8. Ibid., p. 101.

9. Mordecai Paldiel, "Anna Borkowska," in *Encyclopedia of the Holocaust*, vol. 1, ed. in chief Israel Gutman (New York: Macmillan, 1990), p. 233.

10. Silver, p. 102.

Chapter 2. Varian Fry: Assignment: Rescue

1. United States Holocaust Memorial Museum, *Assignment: Rescue, The Story of Varian Fry and the Emergency Rescue Committee* (exhibit program) (Washington, D.C., June 1993–January 1995), p. 1.

2. Mordecai Paldiel, *Sheltering the Jews: Stories of Holocaust Rescuers* (Minneapolis: Fortress Press, 1996), p. 137.

3. Varian Fry, *Assignment: Rescue* (New York: Four Winds Press, 1968), p. 14.

4. Ibid., p. 12.

5. Paldiel, p. 140.

6. Fry, p. 14.

7. United States Holocaust Memorial Museum, p. 5.

8. Paldiel, p. 138.

9. United States Holocaust Memorial Museum, p. 8.

10. Ibid., p. 10.

11. Ibid.

12. Fry, p. 186.

13. "Varian M. Fry, 59, Who Helped Intellectuals Flee Nazis, Is Dead," *The New York Times*, September 14, 1967, p. 47.

14. Paldiel, p. 141.

Chapter 3. Irene Gut Opdyke: Jews Under the Gazebo

1. Gay Block and Malka Drucker, *Rescuers: Portraits of Moral Courage in the Holocaust* (New York: Holmes & Meier, 1992), p. 192.

2. Eva Fogelman, *Conscience & Courage: Rescuers of Jews During the Holocaust* (New York: Doubleday, 1994), p. 49.

3. Ibid., p. 165.

4. Peter Noah, "Heroism in the Holocaust," *Los Angeles Times*, March 11, 1997, p. A3.

5. Ibid.

6. Fogelman, p. 169.

7. Noah, p. A19.

8. Block and Drucker, p. 195.

9. Ibid., p. 196.

10. Ibid.

Chapter 4. Mustafa Hardaga: Muslim Rescuer

1. Ernie Meyer, "First Moslems Honoured as Righteous Gentiles," *Jerusalem Post*, June 17, 1985, p. 3.

2. Eric Silver, *The Book of the Just: The Unsung Heroes Who Rescued Jews from Hitler* (New York: Grove Press, 1992), p. 104.

3. Mordecai Paldiel, *Sheltering the Jews: Stories of Holocaust Rescuers* (Minneapolis: Fortress Press, 1996), p. 72.

4. Silver, p. 105.

5. Meyer, p. 3.

6. Silver, p. 105.

7. Ibid., p. 106.

8. Ibid.

9. Meyer, p. 3.

Chapter 5. Jørgen Kieler: Danish Rescue by Boat

1. Jørgen Kieler, "Jørgen Kieler," in *The Courage to Care: Rescuers of Jews During the Holocaust*, ed. Carol Rittner and Sondra Myers (New York: New York University Press, 1986), p. 86.

2. Ibid., p. 87.

3. Ibid., p. 88.

4. Ibid., p. 89.

5. Ibid.

6. Anna Quindlen, "The Rescuers," *The New York Times*, May 5, 1993, p. A23.

7. Kieler, p. 89.

Chapter 6. Oskar Schindler: Schindler's List

1. Milton Meltzer, *Rescue: The Story of How Gentiles Saved Jews in the Holocaust* (New York: Harper & Row, 1988), p. 56.

2. Ibid., pp. 57–58.

3. Ibid., p. 58.

4. Herbert Steinhouse, "The Man Who Saved a Thousand Lives," in *Oskar Schindler and His List: The Man, the Book, the Film, the Holocaust and Its Survivors*, ed. Thomas Fensch (Forest Dale, Vt.: Paul S. Eriksson, Publisher, 1995), p. 28.

5. Meltzer, p. 66.

6. Ibid.

7. Steinhouse, p. 33.

8. Meltzer, p. 67.

9. Eric Silver, *The Book of the Just: The Unsung Heroes Who Rescued Jews from Hitler* (New York: Grove Press, 1992), p. 148.

Chapter 7. Andrew Sheptitsky: Greek Catholic Rescuer

1. Aharon Weiss, "Andrei Sheptytsky," in *Encyclopedia of the Holocaust*, vol. 4, ed. in chief Israel Gutman (New York: Macmillan, 1990), p. 1347.

2. Ibid., p. 1348.

3. Philip Friedman, *Their Brothers' Keepers* (New York: Holocaust Library, 1978), p. 135.

4. Weiss, p. 1348.

5. Milton Meltzer, *Rescue: The Story of How Gentiles Saved Jews in the Holocaust* (New York: Harper & Row, 1988), p. 43.

6. Martin Gilbert, *The Holocaust: A History of the Jews of Europe During the Second World War* (New York: Holt, Rinehart and Winston, 1985), p. 410.

7. Friedman, pp. 135–136.

8. Weiss, p. 1348.

9. Friedman, p. 135.

Chapter 8. Sempo Sugihara: Japanese Diplomat Rescuer

1. Hillel Levine, *In Search of Sugihara: The Elusive Japanese Diplomat Who Risked His Life to Rescue Ten Thousand Jews from the Holocaust* (New York: Free Press, 1996), p. 124.

2. Ibid., p. 236.

3. Mordecai Paldiel, "Sempo Sugihara," in *Encyclopedia of the Holocaust*, vol. 4, ed. in chief Israel Gutman (New York: Macmillan, 1990), p. 1423.

4. Mordecai Paldiel, *Sheltering the Jews: Stories of Holocaust Rescuers* (Minneapolis: Fortress Press, 1996), p. 141.

5. Levine, pp. 202–203.

6. Ibid., p. 5.

7. Eric Silver, *The Book of the Just: The Unsung Heroes Who Rescued Jews from Hitler* (New York: Grove Press, 1992), p. 38.

8. Levine, p. 7.

9. Ibid., p. 5.

10. Silver, pp. 39–40.

Chapter 9. Marion van Binsbergen Pritchard: Dutch Rescuer of Children

1. Gay Block and Malka Drucker, *Rescuers: Portraits of Moral Courage in the Holocaust* (New York: Holmes & Meier, 1992), p. 33.

2. Ibid.

3. Ibid., p. 34.

4. Eva Fogelman, *Conscience & Courage: Rescuers of Jews During the Holocaust* (New York: Doubleday, 1994), p. 57.

5. Block and Drucker, p. 34.

6. Peter Steinfels, "Beliefs," *The New York Times*, May 12, 1990, p. 11.

7. Block and Drucker, p. 34.

8. Mordecai Paldiel, *Sheltering the Jews: Stories of Holocaust Rescuers* (Minneapolis: Fortress Press, 1996), p. 110.

9. Block and Drucker, pp. 36–37.

10. Fogelman, p. 5.

11. Block and Drucker, p. 38.

12. Ibid., p. 41.

13. Ibid., p. 33.

14. Ibid., p. 40.

Chapter 10. Raoul Wallenberg: "I Want to Save a Nation"

1. Frederick E. Werbell and Clarke Thurston, *Lost Hero: The Mystery of Raoul Wallenberg* (New York: McGraw-Hill, 1982), p. 23.

2. Milton Meltzer, *Rescue: The Story of How Gentiles Saved Jews in the Holocaust* (New York: Harper & Row, 1988), p. 104.

3. Elenore Lester, *Wallenberg: The Man in the Iron Web* (Englewood Cliffs, N.J.: Prentice-Hall, 1982), p. 29.

4. Werbell and Thurston, p. 24.

5. John Bierman, *Righteous Gentile: The Story of Raoul Wallenberg, Missing Hero of the Holocaust*, rev. ed. (New York: Penguin Books, 1995), p. 25.

6. Meltzer, p. 107.

7. Werbell and Thurston, p. 25.

8. Per Anger, *With Raoul Wallenberg in Budapest: Memories of the War Years in Budapest*, trans. David Mel Paul and Margareta Paul (New York: Holocaust Library, 1981), pp. 46–48.

9. Meltzer, p. 108.

10. Bierman, p. 106.

11. Raoul Wallenberg, *Letters and Dispatches, 1924–1944*, trans. Kjersti Board (New York: Arcade Publishing, 1995), p. 246.

12. Meltzer, p.110.

13. Kati Marton, *Wallenberg* (New York: Random House, 1982), p. 111.

14. Meltzer, p.113.

15. Werbell and Thurston, p. 154.

16. Anger, pp. 90–91.

17. Bierman, p. 51.

18. Anger, p. 92.

19. Leni Yahil, "Raoul Wallenberg," in *Encyclopedia of the Holocaust*, vol. 4, ed. in chief Israel Gutman (New York: Macmillan, 1990), p. 1591.

Further Reading

Adler, David. *We Remember the Holocaust.* New York: Henry Holt, 1989.

Altman, Linda Jacobs. *The Holocaust Ghettos.* Springfield, N.J.: Enslow Publishers, Inc., 1998.

Anger, Per. *With Raoul Wallenberg in Budapest: Memories of the War Years in Budapest.* Translated by David Mel Paul and Margareta Paul. New York: Holocaust Library, 1981.

Berenbaum, Michael. *The World Must Know: The History of the Holocaust as Told in the United States Holocaust Memorial Museum.* Boston: Little, Brown and Co., 1993.

Bierman, John. *Righteous Gentile: The Story of Raoul Wallenberg, Missing Hero of the Holocaust.* Rev. ed. New York: Penguin Books, 1995.

Block, Gay, and Malka Drucker. *Rescuers: Portraits of Moral Courage in the Holocaust.* New York: Holmes & Meier, 1992.

Brecher, Elinor J. *Schindler's Legacy: True Stories of the List Survivors.* New York: Dutton Books, 1994.

Byers, Ann. *The Holocaust Camps.* Springfield, N.J.: Enslow Publishers, Inc., 1998.

Dawidowicz, Lucy S. *The War Against the Jews, 1933–1945.* 10th anniversary ed. New York: Seth Press, 1986.

Fensch, Thomas, ed. *Oskar Schindler and His List: The Man, the Book, the Film, the Holocaust and Its Survivors.* Forest Dale, Vt.: Paul S. Eriksson, Publisher, 1995.

Flender, Harold. *Rescue in Denmark.* New York: Simon & Schuster, 1963.

Fogelman, Eva. *Conscience & Courage: Rescuers of Jews During the Holocaust.* New York: Doubleday, 1994.

Frank, Anne. *Anne Frank: The Diary of a Young Girl.* New York: Doubleday, 1967.

Fremon, David K. *The Holocaust Heroes.* Springfield, N.J.: Enslow Publishers, Inc., 1998.

Friedman, Ina R. *Escape or Die: True Stories of Young People Who Survived the Holocaust.* Reading, Mass.: Addison-Wesley, 1982.

Friedman, Philip. *Their Brothers' Keepers.* New York: Holocaust Library, 1978.

Fry, Varian. *Assignment: Rescue.* New York: Four Winds Press, 1968.

Gilbert, Martin. *The Holocaust: A History of the Jews of Europe During the Second World War.* New York: Holt, Rinehart and Winston, 1985.

Greenfeld, Howard. *The Hidden Children.* New York: Ticknor & Fields, 1993.

Gutman, Israel, ed. in chief. *Encyclopedia of the Holocaust.* 4 vols. New York: Macmillan, 1990.

Holliday, Laurel. *Children in the Holocaust and World War II: Their Secret Diaries.* New York: Washington Square Press, 1995.

Keneally, Thomas. *Schindler's List.* New York: Simon & Schuster, 1982.

Leboucher, Fernande. *Incredible Mission.* Garden City, N.Y.: Doubleday, 1969.

Lester, Elenore. *Wallenberg: The Man in the Iron Web.* Englewood Cliffs, N.J.: Prentice-Hall, 1982.

Levine, Hillel. *In Search of Sugihara: The Elusive Japanese Diplomat Who Risked His Life to Rescue Ten Thousand Jews from the Holocaust.* New York: Free Press, 1996.

Linnéa, Sharon. *Raoul Wallenberg: The Man Who Stopped Death.* Philadelphia: The Jewish Publication Society, 1993.

Marton, Kati. *Wallenberg.* New York: Random House, 1982.

Meltzer, Milton. *Rescue: The Story of How Gentiles Saved Jews in the Holocaust.* New York: Harper & Row, 1988.

Paldiel, Mordecai. *The Path of the Righteous: Gentile Rescuers of Jews During the Holocaust.* Hoboken, N.J.: KTAV Publishing House, 1993.

———. *Sheltering the Jews: Stories of Holocaust Rescuers.* Minneapolis: Fortress Press, 1996.

Rittner, Carol, and Sondra Myers, eds. *The Courage to Care: Rescuers of Jews During the Holocaust.* New York: New York University Press, 1986.

Rogasky, Barbara. *Smoke and Ashes: The Story of the Holocaust.* New York: Holiday House, 1988.

Silver, Eric. *The Book of the Just: The Unsung Heroes Who Rescued Jews from Hitler.* New York: Grove Press, 1992.

United States Holocaust Memorial Museum. *Assignment: Rescue, The Story of Varian Fry and the Emergency Committee.* Exhibit program. Washington, D.C., June 1993–January 1995.

Wallenberg, Raoul. *Letters and Dispatches, 1924–1944.* Translated by Kjersti Board. New York: Arcade Publishing, 1995.

Werbell, Frederick E., and Thurston Clarke. *Lost Hero: The Mystery of Raoul Wallenberg.* New York: McGraw-Hill, 1982.

Yeatts, Tabatha. *The Holocaust Survivors.* Springfield, N.J.: Enslow Publishers, Inc., 1998.

Internet Addresses

The Anne Frank House
<http://www.annefrank.nl>
> A virtual tour of Anne Frank's hiding place, a complete text of her famous diary, biographical details of her life, and historical information about the Holocaust in the Netherlands.

United States Holocaust Memorial Museum
<http://www.ushmm.org>
> Provides links and mailing addresses to an extensive list of Holocaust organizations.

Simon Wiesenthal Center
<http://www.wiesenthal.com>
> This international center for Holocaust remembrance and the defense of human rights houses an extensive library of Holocaust and genocide information.

Yad Vashem
<http://www.yad-vashem.org.il>
> The national Holocaust memorial of Israel collects and shares documents, photographs, and studies of the Holocaust.

Index

About the Author

Darryl Lyman has written many educational and musical works for young people. His books for adult readers include collective biographies of Jewish cultural figures and collections of Civil War quotations. This is his first book for Enslow Publishers, Inc.